EVERY AUSTRALIAN COUNTS

EVERY AUSTRALIAN COUNTS

THE BIRTH OF THE NDIS

MICHAEL EPIS
WITH ANITA PHILLIPS

MELBOURNE
UNIVERSITY
PRESS

MELBOURNE UNIVERSITY PRESS
An imprint of Melbourne University Publishing Limited
Level 1, 715 Swanston Street, Carlton, Victoria 3053, Australia
mup-contact@unimelb.edu.au
www.mup.com.au

First published 2023
Text © National Disability Insurance Agency, 2023
Design and typography © Melbourne University Publishing Limited, 2023

 A catalogue record for this book is available from the National Library of Australia

Every attempt has been made to locate the copyright holders for material quoted in this book. Any person or organisation that may have been overlooked or misattributed may contact the publisher.

Cover design by Philip Campbell Design
Typeset by Adala Studio
Cover image: Photographer unknown, reproduced courtesy Every Australian Counts.

9780522880175 (paperback)
9780522880182 (ebook)

CONTENTS

———

Dr Anita Frances Phillips first suggested the idea for this book, which draws in part on interviews conducted for her PhD, 'The process of policy development using the NDIS as a case study'.

Dr Phillips was a former member of the Queensland Parliament who passed away early in 2023, not long after this book was underway. She was a trailblazer for women in politics and a true champion of the NDIS.

She is survived by her daughters Rebecca, Melanie and Keinton.

THE SCENE IS SET

———

THERE WERE 1002 delegates gathered in the Great Hall of Parliament House, Canberra.

It was April 2008 and the Labor government was riding high.

Not quite five months into its first term, its members and its prime minister, Kevin Rudd, were still aglow as the government continued to ride the wave that had brought Labor to power after eleven years in opposition.

The Apology that had been promised to Indigenous Australians as a matter of priority had been delivered at the first available opportunity, in the most appropriate forum, on the first day of the new parliament. It had been cleansing and healing—the nation was both humbled and enlarged by the simple act of telling the truth, acknowledging the past and saying sorry.

And now, once again in Parliament House, which beckoned in a larger democracy than did its charming but limited predecessor, was a new adventure. The Australia 2020 Summit.

Just over a thousand people from across the country, chosen for their expertise and experience, for their demography and geography, for their smarts and hearts, had gathered together to offer up their ideas of what Australia should do to be the country it should be come 2020.

They had come from far and wide, and reflected the diverse nation Australia had become.

The whole show was the brainchild of Rudd, a man who seemed to have a natural affinity with ideas, whose capacity to speak in sentences that had multiple subclauses still retained some sort of charm. New adventure it may have been, but everyone was conscious that the summit aped a previous gathering, the 1983 National Economic Summit of Bob Hawke's then-new government, which put in place the Prices and Incomes Accord, under which unions and business negotiated and cooperated for a newer, better Australia.

'Today we are trying to do something new,' Rudd said in his opening address.

'Today we are throwing open the windows of our democracy, to let a little bit of fresh air in.

'Rather than pretending that we the politicians of Australia have all the answers, and the truth is, we don't, we are turning now to you, the people of Australia.'

His address over, the delegates broke into their groups and set about arguing their ideas.

So it was that Kevin Rudd was led into a room that sunny morning by one of the new boys of the Class of 07, Bill Shorten, who, much to his surprise, had been appointed parliamentary secretary for disability and children's services. In the room were twenty-odd people discussing how to improve life for families and communities.

Tanya Plibersek—by this stage an experienced hand, and the relevant minister—motioned to Ahmed Fahour, the then head of the National Australia Bank, who argued the case for a social impact fund. Shorten knew what was coming next. Rudd didn't.

Shorten glanced at Plibersek, who motioned to a woman to take the floor. She rose and, in the couple of minutes available to her, told the prime minister that what this country needed was something a bit like Medicare, and a bit like superannuation—an insurance scheme, in which everyone paid a small amount and everyone was insured against disability. That is, if you were born with a disability, or one developed, or if you had an accident, you were insured—help would be provided and the cost of living with disability covered. It was needed, said Gina Anderson, the woman speaking, because those people were suffering, due to the fact that, in most cases, the government didn't provide for them, and their families paid the cost. What we need, said Gina, is a National Disability Insurance Scheme.

The room approved. Prime Minister Rudd nodded, and thanked Gina for her contribution.

Bill Shorten seized the day, and then the butcher's paper, on which he scrawled *Establish an NDIS*.

OUT OF SIGHT, OUT OF MIND

———

ONCE UPON A time, hundreds of thousands of Australians were forced to live in institutions, where all the exercising of free will that a person expects in life was denied them. They had no rights. None.

These people had done nothing wrong, yet they were not allowed beyond the boundaries of the institutions in which they were kept. This implies that they could not work, although many did work inside the institutions, but only for token wages. And if these people had been paid wages, they likely couldn't buy anything anyway, not being allowed out. These people were kept locked up, but they were fed and sheltered. They had no choice, however, over their food, which was served along institutional lines—at regimented times, in regimented portions, in regimented patterns. Sometimes they were not fed enough. These people had no choice over where they were sheltered, which further implies that they had no choice over who they lived with.

These people lived in institutions where they were detained indefinitely. Many, as a result, became institutionalised: having been denied free will throughout their lives, they often lost the capability to exercise it, if and when it ever became available.

These institutions often became a law unto themselves. They were places of incarceration, of discipline and regimentation, of orders and

4

commands, of the lock and key—and thus, places of shadows, where abuse, be it sexual, financial, psychological, physical or any other you might nominate, could thrive. Too often, it did.

Who were these people?

They were people with disability.

And when was this time?

Not that long ago—up until the last decade of the twentieth century.

They were people with an intellectual disability. Or a physical disability. Or a mental illness. Which meant an extremely intelligent person with cerebral palsy might have been bunking in a dormitory next to a person with schizophrenia, next to someone else who has dementia. Or polio. Those people, as we see clearly now, have nothing in common—except for the fact that Australian society saw them all as a problem to be solved. Even, perhaps, a problem to be moved out of sight, and thus out of mind. If they were provided with food and shelter, that was deemed to be enough—problem solved. Rehabilitation, treatment, support—they were not on the menu.

These institutions were a nineteenth-century creation, and thus created according to nineteenth-century thinking. Mental illness, for example, was more often than not regarded as incurable—which made treatment redundant. Likewise, the notion of early intervention when it came to intellectual impairment was also not in play. That thinking was written into the names of these places, such as 'Kew Idiot Asylum'; 'the Home for Incurables', in Adelaide; and the contradiction in terms of Melbourne's 'Austin Hospital for Incurables'. There was also a 'Colony for Epileptics'. Note the terminology—'asylum', 'colony'. That is, places to shut people away from the rest of society. Sounds rather like prison, doesn't it? But a prisoner usually gets released, and lives with foreknowledge of the date of that release.

These institutions were usually located in the countryside, for various reasons: because fresh air was considered beneficial to the patients' health; because the land was cheaper; because, that way, the patients were out of sight and out of mind.

The release of those considered mentally ill began in the 1960s and continued through the 1970s. This was borne upon a wave of realisation that treatment could work, and that destigmatisation—by moving people back into the general community and moving their treatment into general hospitals—would aid in rehabilitation. Advances in pharmaceuticals accelerated the process, so that the 30 000 beds that accommodated the mentally ill in the 1960s dwindled into the thousands come the turn of the century.

Those with disability had to wait longer.

Things began to change in 1981, the year that the United Nations had deemed the International Year of Disabled Persons. The UN had announced this designation five years in advance, and the groundswell for securing the rights of the disabled had made itself felt in the meantime. The UN declared that the purpose of the year was to bring about 'full participation and equality' for those people, so that they could participate fully in their societies, and enjoy all life has to offer, just like anyone else.

That year, 1981, was also the year the then prime minister, Malcolm Fraser, inaugurated Australia's Human Rights Commission, which took up the cause of these people.

That was the year the Disability Resources Centre was established in Brunswick, Melbourne, run by people with disability, informing others of their rights and the services available. One of its founders was advocate Lesley Hall, who, with fellow activists, stormed the stage at St Kilda Town Hall in Melbourne during the Miss Australia pageant as the contestants paraded. They were protesting against the inherent contradiction of that celebration of physical beauty being run by the Spastic Society of Victoria, raising money for the disability service provider Yooralla.

That was the year the federal minister for social services was presented with a bill of rights by the Victorian Association of Intellectually Disadvantaged Citizens (later to become Reinforce).

Two years later, Australia had a new prime minister, Bob Hawke, and his government addressed, more urgently and more closely than any previous government, the situation of those with disability. It established the Disability Advisory Council of Australia.

The result, two years and two months later—after the government received 1700 submissions, after it involved more than 5000 people in public consultations in sixty-five locations across the country—was *New Directions*, a comprehensive and thoughtful document that set a fresh course.

'In recent years people with disabilities have begun to speak out and be heard in the Australian community, both as individuals and through consumer organisations and self-help groups,' it began. 'They have made it clear that they want to be treated as people first—people whose abilities matter more than their disabilities. They do not want to be seen as sick or different and they do not want all decisions to be made for them by other people.'

And, for the first time, people with a disability had a say—making numerous submissions to the inquiry.

New Directions took its task seriously. Its 146 pages said all the right things. Those pages marked a change in language—it referenced its 'Handicapped Programs Review', noting that the term would no longer be used. 'Disabled' was the new term, which was often interchangeable with 'consumer', at the time a term redeployed by government for those receiving its services.

The government's focus was on how to get people out of institutions and into independent living; on getting people training to improve their employment prospects; on ensuring access to public services, such as transport and education.

It faced the hard facts: 250 000 people were experiencing extreme disadvantage. When services were provided, they were provided unevenly—and 'unevenly' had a very slippery meaning. 'In some areas there is a lack of services at all,' *New Directions* noted.

The government determined to change things: 'to move the focus from programs to individual consumer outcomes', 'to facilitate the integration of people with disabilities into general community activities', to ensure equity by allocating funds on the basis of need. It recommended anti-discrimination legislation, the establishment of an Office of Disability, and the immediate appointment to the Human Rights Commission of someone with the sole purpose of examining such discrimination. It embraced 'the fundamental right that all people are of equal worth'. The result the next year was the Disability Services Act, which gave force to many of the report's recommendations.

These were heady times. The prospects for people with disability were much better than they had ever been. Hope flourished.

ᔐ

In Victoria, Aradale, as it had come to be known, was one of these institutions. Taking four years to build, it opened in 1867, within a week of another such institution, Beechworth Lunatic Asylum. The names are indicative of a different time and different thinking: Aradale had been known sequentially as the Ararat Lunatic Asylum, Ararat Hospital for the Insane and the Ararat Mental Hospital. 'Asylum' indicated at the time that the institution was a place of detention. In the first decade of the nineteenth century, these places had their names changed to 'hospitals'—but that did not mean what went on within their walls changed a great deal.

Both Ararat and Beechworth housed a number of those who had ventured to Australia to make their fortune in the gold rush—and failed. Both places were far from the capital. Ararat had slowly been emptied in the first stage of deinstitutionalisation, its 800 beds in the 1960s becoming just 245 come 1991. That was the year the Victorian government received from Ben Bodna, the Public Advocate (a position created care of the Disability Services Act) a recommendation to investigate goings-on at Aradale. By this time, it was home mainly to those with intellectual disability, and to those in its psychiatric hospital, some of whom were deemed criminally insane, detained in separate premises known as J Ward.

The investigation found that the average stay for a psychiatric patient was more than twenty-two years—a shockingly long time. There were 245 residents and 455 staff. That looks like a resident–staff ratio that others could only dream of, yet the residents were locked in overnight, with minimal supervision or care—all the wards were locked. Indeed, as resident numbers were decreasing, staff numbers were increasing. The cost per client was $70 000 a year—double the cost in an aged care facility. Anywhere up to half of the food purchased never actually made it on to the plates of residents. In fact, they were underfed. They were in poor health, many with rotting teeth. They had no privacy, sleeping in 20-bed wards. There were no private toilets—the building was constructed like soldiers' barracks. Their money was lost, stolen or misused. They were denied recreation. They were denied social workers, occupational therapists and psychologists. One resident engaged in prostitution. Allegations of rape had not been investigated properly by staff.

In short, the residents were abused. They were being abused systemically, at scale. The institution was being run not for their benefit, but for the benefit of those employed there, who had a vested interest in maintaining the dependency of those in their charge. This was five years after the Disability Services Act, six years after *New Directions*, ten years after the International Year of Disabled Persons.

Aradale was shut down.

The era of the institutions was over.

For many in the disability sector, this was a time of exultation. The closure of Aradale was, indeed, to be celebrated.

One person caught up in the first flush of excitement about what could be achieved was Rhonda Galbally, who, a few years earlier, in 1983, had been CEO of the Myer Foundation and Sidney Myer Fund, two philanthropic organisations founded by the Myer department store family. One of Galbally's first tasks in the role had been to oversee a grant for the first disabled group home in Australia, initiated by the actor Nancy Black and her partner, Playbox Theatre Company founder Carrillo Gantner, for their daughter Cassie. 'It was seen as revolutionary to have a homely place for Cassie with a small group of other disabled people,' Galbally later recalled.

In her 2016 Sambell Oration, named for a former director of the Brotherhood of St Laurence, Galbally said: 'While mental institutions had existed since the late nineteenth century, the response to the polio epidemic heralded the emergence of places similar to asylums that would contain people with disabilities for their entire lives—away from shame and fear and from the dangers of the outside world. Not only did institutions provide a solution about what to do with the sudden flood of cripples, they were places where having a disability was the absolute focus. In institutions, disability was all-encompassing—the definition of identity. This is instead of being a person, where having a disability is just another characteristic, like brown eyes. Because disability dominated in institutions, aspirations were minimal in relation to critical areas for living, such as education to the maximum with employment as the aim. And because institutions looked after people with disability far away from the world, the world remained seriously and actively handicapping, with inaccessible and unwelcoming built environments and attitudes—including in schools, communities and workplaces.'

For that reason, Galbally, like so many others, welcomed deinstitutionalisation.

'Because we did not have the legislative springboard of a Bill of Rights ... we in Australia were slower and ultimately less successful in forcing mainstream systems such as health, education, transport and buildings to include people with disabilities compared with the USA, Canada, Sweden, Netherlands, Germany and the UK.

'We were, however, successful in fighting to close institutions. We saw those institutions ... as the symbol of all that was wrong with disability, with people locked away from society, out of sight and out of mind. Deinstitutionalisation became our main aim, and we certainly were responsible for reducing the number of institutions in Australia. We celebrated as a major win the replacement of institutions with community residential units or group homes. Because they only had six to eight residents, we thought this was a vast improvement on three hundred or even sixty.'

The initial experience of many released from institutions was wonderful. Suddenly, they had a sense of freedom. You could look from your bedroom window and see people walking in the streets, rather than seeing the imprisoning institutional walls. You could, maybe, rise late and, maybe, have a breakfast that you chose at a time that you chose. You might even be able to catch a bus and spend a day at your local library, for example, reading books that had never been made available to you, opening up worlds whose existence you could never have suspected.

Galbally recalls that 'the 1990s saw the beginnings of accessible transport and accessible government buildings. There were flurries around inclusive playgroups and childcare. But basically, getting governments to mandate the move towards inclusive mainstream systems and infrastructure was piecemeal and painful—one step forward and two back. For example, special schools kept making a resurgence even though all of the evidence, even at that stage, showed that mainstream education brings superior learning outcomes for disabled children.'

Likewise with health: 'Some systems remained untouched, like health where still, every day, people with disabilities are denied access and treatment for conditions unrelated to their disability.'

Overall, though, for many, most of the time, the new ways were better.

One survey of the literature of deinstitutionalisation found many benefits in the first years. Adaptive behaviour by those who had been released was much improved. Lifestyle choices—where to go, what to do—were greatly expanded. Quality of life was generally greater, as measured by people having the opportunity to expand their boundaries. Activity levels, skills acquired, community participation, leisure activities—all seemed to be better than previously.

But ... the gains plateaued very quickly.

Within a few short years, few, if any, further gains were being made.

And the problems, which had been overlooked in the first rush of enthusiasm, were becoming all too apparent.

Deinstitutionalisation quickly became reinstitutionalisation.

Care 'in the community' all too quickly became care 'by the community'—where 'community' all too often meant mum and dad.

For many of the mentally ill, the new institution *was* a prison. Literally. Likewise for those with acquired brain injuries or intellectual impairment.

People found that living in a house with three or four others—you still did not have a choice who they would be—could be just as bad as, and even worse than, a large institution. You lived cheek by jowl with your housemates—inmates? In the institutions, there had at least been space.

In 1993 came the release of the Burdekin Report, named for the then federal human rights commissioner, Brian Burdekin, who had inquired into the rights of those with mental illness. On releasing the report, he said, 'the inquiry established that the policy of deinstitutionalisation has largely failed—and that it will not succeed until it is accompanied by appropriate policies on housing—and an adequate allocation of resources'.

Having been released from the institutions that held them, all too many of the mentally ill had ended up homeless, in jail, in shelters and refuges, in boarding houses. As had those with brain injuries; indeed, they still do—it is estimated that up to half of Australia's male prison population has a brain injury.

Four years earlier, in 1989, Burdekin had given the Kenneth Jenkins Oration, named for the revered disability advocate. Burdekin had enumerated the rights of the disabled person, as defined by the United Nations and agreed to by Australia: the right to dignity, to a decent life, to treatment and rehabilitation, to productive employment, to family life, to economic and social security, to protection against discrimination. 'We in Australia have a long way to go,' he concluded. He was right.

∽

For many of the intellectually impaired, the new institution they were condemned to was their family home. For many of their parents and carers, the family home had become their prison too.

For many of those with disability, their new institution was their communal house. They still did not get to choose who they lived with, who they saw, where they could go—all the normal things you expect from life.

Galbally was among those dismayed by how things turned out.

'Everyone thought group homes were fabulous at the time, but had no understanding that institutional care was simply transferred across to group homes—for example, Cassie's home.

'It was very dismaying to realise several years later that group homes can also fast become institutional, providing no tenancy rights or choice over who you live with, how you spend your day, what you eat and for most residents seeing no non-disabled people except paid workers,' she later recalled.

'Other models that were also supported in part by philanthropy were also similar to institutions: segregated and closed. For example, adult day programs spread across Australia, and they were often like kindergartens: institution-like places to fill in time that treated people with disabilities like infants. People were shut off from the outside world, occasionally going out into the world in large groups for recreation where interaction and opportunities to make friends with non-disabled people were not possible.'

The situation had not improved in regard to employment either.

'Sheltered workshops were segregated institutions, paying below-minimum wages, and with perverse business models with incentives to retain the most productive workers to make the business more profitable, rather than encouraging them to transition into mainstream employment.'

Another big problem was emerging: the duties carried out by parents now caring for their children at home.

John Della Bosca was the New South Wales minister for disability services in 2003. He encountered the problem firsthand.

'There was a bit of a political crisis happening within the NSW disability system, which was generated by ... "respite block". Basically, once deinstitutionalisation happened, there was a big liability put back onto families and the trade-off for that was adequate respite. The contract was to try to offer adequate respite so that families could have some break from the caring responsibilities. And of course, what would happen, especially with children, is that people would get to the point where they couldn't cope anymore for a variety of reasons, and they'd leave, or just abandon the child literally.'

Yes, caring for their children, with little or no support, could become so onerous for parents, many of them aged and infirm themselves, that they would abandon them while in care.

'And that would mean that places ... were blocked for other families and then that would just become like a Disney experiment of a nuclear explosion with ping-pong balls going off all around the room, letting off mouse traps,' Della Bosca says.

'And more and more families going into crisis, and more and more respite blocks and so on. We just hadn't invested enough; when I say we, the whole community hadn't invested enough way back when deinstitutionalisation started.

'Deinstitutionalisation became an excuse for treasuries to reduce the exposure of public expenditure to disability, and what it should have been doing was transferring resources into the community. Instead they just limited the resources to stuff like respite, which is really just a very small part of a much bigger picture of support that should have been there.'

Della Bosca asked an actuary he worked with, John Walsh, to look over what data was available in relation to disability spending and disability need. What Walsh found was disturbing.

'The system of deinstitutionalisation meant most money went into supported accommodation [group homes] for a limited number of people, with little community support financially to support families—the system was not equitable, nor sustainable,' says Walsh. About 5 per cent of people were taking 80 per cent of funding. Walsh ran the calculations, and could see demand outstripping spending by 7 to 10 per cent above inflation into the foreseeable future.

'Families were getting older and there were increasing instances where persons with disability were in fact abandoned to the state because their families were unable to continue to provide support for them. Each of these cases required an emergency entry into a supported accommodation place, which was a very expensive option. But because of the rationed funding, this in turn drew even more money from the rationed system and reduced even further the availability of community support. So, the system was in what could be considered a death spiral.'

The equation was simple, said Walsh: demand far outstripped supply. And demand was growing exponentially.

Back in 1985, the *New Directions* report had included a tucked-away little sentence, referring to those who had made submissions: 'Some people referred to likely resource impediments to the immediate implementation of all these policies.'

That was the gentle understatement of polite bureaucratese. Further on, however, more blunt language emerged: 'It would be unrealistic, however, to expect that resources would be available immediately to satisfy all needs.'

Those words had turned out to be all too true.

The closure of the institutions had created a whole raft of new problems. Before they could be solved, they first had to be uncovered, detailed, itemised. And to be fixed, they had to be funded. That loomed as the biggest problem of all. If funding wasn't fixed, nothing would be fixed.

THE HIDDEN CITY

———

QUEENSLAND LABOR SENATOR Jan McLucas had tried for several years to have an inquiry into the disability sector. In 2006 she succeeded. McLucas had a general idea of what the inquiry would find—but wasn't quite prepared for what it did find.

'It's a long time ago now, but some stories just stay with you. We heard evidence from a woman in Tasmania,' McLucas recalls, her voice lowering. 'She was about thirty-five; from memory, she had MS; and she was stuck in an aged care home. She said, "I stopped making friends here with the old people in the nursing home because they just die."

'I remember meeting a mum and her ten-year-old in Brisbane one day at a cerebral palsy group. This little fellow was in a wheelchair. He was not due for a replacement wheelchair until he was thirteen. The rule in Queensland was you could only get a wheelchair every five years. The physiotherapist had said that the damage the wheelchair was causing to the boy's spine—not the cerebral palsy, the wheelchair—was going to disable him further by the time his new wheelchair was due. Heartbreaking, just heartbreaking.'

McLucas had known the situation for people with disability was bad—but it was important to quantify through an inquiry just how bad it was. Part of the motivation, she explains, was that developing policy is difficult in opposition; an inquiry not only flushes out detail, but expert submissions and the testimony of people in the system provide granular detail of where things are going astray. And, perhaps, can point the way forward.

Her initial efforts to get an inquiry had been stymied by the Coalition government. There are times when those in government don't want to find a problem—because they have no appetite to fix it. It's just not on their agenda. And maybe they know, or suspect, that the problem is so big, so ugly, that it is going to take a lot of fixing. The situation was similar then: 'The view at the time was that disability services are delivered by the states and territories. Got nothing to do with us [the commonwealth]. We give you a bit of money. And that's it,' says McLucas.

Eventually, however, she succeeded in getting the problem investigated, which she puts down to ceaseless haranguing of the politicians by the disability sector. 'And, also, it's a bit hard to keep saying, "No, we don't want to talk about disability."'

In 2004 McLucas had been appointed shadow minister for disability services. One thing she knew was that the situation in Queensland was particularly bad.

'I'm from Queensland, and I vividly recall then-premier Joh Bjelke-Petersen saying, "We don't have people with disabilities in Queensland." That was the attitude then—we don't have disability, because the parent of the disabled child was the carer, with sole responsibility. That was the mind-set in Queensland, which was appalling. [Premier] Anna Bligh doubled spending on disability one year, and Queensland was still running last.'

In February 2007 the Senate's Standing Committee on Community Affairs tabled its report on disability funding. Not simply the amount of funding, not simply who got the funding, not simply how the funding was allocated—rather, *everything* about funding.

The job was done properly, with more than sixty witnesses appearing at hearings held in the capital cities, culminating in a comprehensive 171-page report, which listed twenty-nine recommendations.

At the time, the Howard government was about to embark on the fourth iteration of the Commonwealth State/Territory Disability Agreement (CSTDA), the mechanism by which the commonwealth and states funded disability. Some of the funding was provided by the commonwealth, all of it was spent by the states. This model of funding was introduced in 1991, in response to the *New Directions* report and deinstitutionalisation, and it was the object of the committee's inquiry.

The inquiry was empowered to examine how well the intent of the three previous agreements had been achieved; the appropriateness of the funding agreements, with attention to unmet needs, especially accommodation and services; and alternative modes of funding, jurisdiction and administrative arrangements.

McLucas, who sat on the committee, has one word to describe the funding model: begging.

'You know, as minister for disabilities in the states, you would go with your begging bowl to the treasurer, and say, "Please, can I have those crumbs that are about to fall off the side of your table?" That was the hopelessness of the funding model. It was the begging-bowl approach. Rather than saying "This is the population of people with disabilities, this is the nature of their disabilities, we've done an assessment of what it costs over a lifetime, these are their ages, et cetera, so that the cost for supporting people with disability in our state will be this figure". And it's not that hard a thing to do, the actuarial approach.'

McLucas's eyes were quickly opened when she took on that shadow portfolio. 'People were coming to visit me and telling me how terrible things were. While everyone knew that the disability sector and the funding of disability was broken, they [the Coalition government] just did not want the focus of a Senate inquiry to that extent at that time.

It took three goes of me moving that we would have this inquiry, until finally the Liberals agreed.'

While McLucas knew things were bad in Queensland, the sheer fact that each state did things its own way in delivering services was its own problem.

'In every state and territory, it was a different model—in some, it was a devolved model where NFPs [not-for-profits] provided services; in others, it was government-delivered services. There were different levels of trepidation from people with disability, because Victoria's model wasn't too bad. And they also had a bit of a personal individual model for some people as well. And so did Western Australia.'

One effect of this federal model was a lack of transportability between states—if you moved from, say, Victoria to South Australia, it was just a matter of luck whether you would be funded to the same degree, whether the same services would be available, and so on. And you would have to go through the application process all over again—and there was no reason to believe the criteria in one state would even resemble the criteria in another state. Naturally, you went to the back of the queue.

All of this had serious effects—who would want to move interstate and go through that process all over again? Without anyone ever stopping to think through the consequences, the model had already placed a severe limitation on the lives of people with disability, by throwing in their path a huge disincentive ever to move. That disincentive was borne, of course, by their parents or partners or carers, or a combination thereof, who likewise were encumbered with this disincentive to move interstate for that more attractive job. As one private individual submitted to the inquiry: 'You are not a citizen of Australia. You are only a citizen of the state in which you live.' Queensland ALP senator Claire Moore was the committee deputy chair. She describes the situation succinctly: 'Borders often determined what support people would get.'

The first, but not primary, recommendation the report made was that state and territory governments create a specific service to ease the transition for a person moving interstate.

$\backsim$

The sector's voices carried the message loud and clear, day in and day out, that the greatest problem was underfunding.

Documented evidence in the form of international tables made it clear that among countries in the Organisation for Economic Co-operation and Development (OECD), Australia's spending on disability per capita was about the lowest in the developed world. What was not documented, as McLucas alluded to above, was the unmet need—it was not at all clear exactly what *was* needed, because no comprehensive effort had ever been made to find out.

The report that came from McLucas's urgings for an inquiry echoed this—of its twenty-nine recommendations, it elevated fixing insufficient funding above all else.

The inquiry took a historical perspective, looking back to the evolution of the sector. The funding mechanism currently in place—the CSTDA—was the eventual outcome of work done by the Hawke government in 1983. *New Directions* had set out the framework for reform, especially the funding mechanism, the services provided and the purpose of those services. It resulted in the Disability Services Act 1986, whose purpose was to reduce the dependence on charity and welfare models of service provision, and to find ways to promote independent living in the community (that is, not in institutions).

New Directions had pinpointed very specific problems, particularly the lack of cohesion between commonwealth and state actions, which resulted in the dual sins of duplication and gaps in coverage, the lack of specified objectives in so many programs and services, and a lack of focus on the person receiving the service. The recipient was almost an afterthought in the scheme of things. An inconvenience, even.

One major outcome of the Act was that the commonwealth took responsibility for employment services and labour market programs, while responsibility for accommodation, community support, community access, respite and other support services fell to the states.

The principle that people with disability had 'the same basic human rights as other members of Australian society' had existed since *New Directions*, but the practice fell a long way short of the theory. The notion of having rights collided head on with the funding: when the money ran out, you had no rights.

The Disability Services Agreement had been introduced by the Hawke government to reform the sector, and had been succeeded by the Commonwealth State Disability Agreement (CSDA—eventually CSTDA, the 'T' standing for 'territories'). The CSTDA was meant to fix the inadequacies of its predecessor; particularly, to define more clearly the roles and responsibilities of the various jurisdictions in delivering specialist disability services. By the late 1990s, when that model was well underway, differences in service provision across the various states were causing concern. Parents and carers, especially, were expressing their dissatisfaction and their need for additional support in their caring roles. The CSTDA called for increased accountability of states and territories for their spending. It stressed the importance of implementing strategies with a 'consumer focus', to use its terminology, particularly in services such as accommodation, in-home care and other support services. The overall aim was for greater consistency and comparability nationally; not only with regard to geographic regions but also to disability groups and services, as there was evidence of considerable variance between funding and services available for different categories of disability. However, in less than ten years from the commencement of this program, different states and territories were interpreting its implementation within their own unique political, economic or geographical environments, and developing quite different services and programs.

In 1996 a review of the first CSTDA, which ran from 1991, found that there were no means by which governments could converse to plan and develop the service system, nor to coordinate the separate service provision by the two levels of government. Most disturbingly, there was no way to measure unmet demand—which is another way of saying the system was flying blind. Lastly, it did little, if anything, to meet the needs of carers—read 'mum and dad'—which were extensive to the point of being overwhelming. That was 1996. By 2007 the same problems still existed, but had worsened.

Different programs being run by the different states made comparisons between them all but impossible. Further, they made interface with the commonwealth bewilderingly complex. That complexity was even worse at ground level for those seeking aid, who faced a constant merry-go-round in accessing services. Bureaucracy was eating up the lives not just of those administering the various available schemes but of those trying to access them.

Tasmanian Anglicare submitted to the 2007 inquiry a dismaying example of one person's experience: ' "Well, it took us fourteen years to find out that we could get assistance with shoes"... There is no one point of information for people to go to.' The Tasmanian submission continued, 'They may go to one agency and get a bit of the picture, and they go to another agency and get another bit of the picture. But there is no one point that can give them a picture of all the services they might be entitled to.'

Bureaucracies are by nature difficult, and become more difficult when multiple bureaucracies overlap. Everyone knows that experience of one office saying to you the other office is responsible; after interminable delays, when you contact the second office, it says no, the first office is the responsible party. Weeks or months have passed, and you are back at square one—behind square one, even; demoralised and angry.

Complex systems throw up anomalies too. For instance, the committee found that in Victoria, a person could apply for financial aid to
buy a wheelchair. But if that person was, for example, discharged from
a hospital into supported accommodation—say, a nursing home—they
were ineligible for a wheelchair. That person could then find themselves
in a catch-22: if they had a wheelchair, they could return home. But they
could not get the wheelchair, because they had to be living at home to
qualify for the wheelchair. Moving home and then applying for a wheelchair was not an option if you could not move at all—and, anyway, the
wheelchair might be years in coming. The lack of coordination between
governments, and lack of cohesion in piecemeal allocations, engendered
these bureaucratic nightmares, making difficult lives all the more
difficult.

The committee found that the provision of assisted technology—
things like wheelchairs and hoists—was a major shortcoming in meeting
the needs of the disabled. Such goods were not covered at all in the
CSTDA, despite the fact that nearly half of all people with disabilities
use some assistive technology. The Australian Institute of Health and
Welfare (AIHW) suggested that aids and equipment alone could often
be more effective than personal assistance.

The lack of a hoist to enable an elderly carer to get their loved one
in and out of bed was enough to mean a permanent bed in, say, an aged
care facility would have to be found, at far greater cost to the system.
The provision of such aids was different in every state, with a lot of the
providing still being done by charitable organisations, not government.

One man, aged forty-two and living in cluster-style accommodation,
said he was, in effect, living in solitary confinement because his condition had deteriorated and he could no longer move himself around in
his manual wheelchair but needed an electric one. He said he spent most
of his time watching daytime TV, because he could not get himself to
his bedroom to access his computer. Often, people had to pay half of

the then $10 000 cost for an electric wheelchair—money that many did not have. The cruel irony of billions of dollars being spent on disability services but a person's life being wasted because of the lack of a few thousand dollars was lost on no one.

AIHW estimated that the unmet needs for equipment of those with cerebral palsy was around $4 million—a comparatively small figure that would vastly improve the quality of life for many people.

One submission pointed out a horrible fact. The person's wheelchair was provided by Queensland Health: 'If I moved to another state I would have to hand the chair back.'

Not providing the aid equipment in the first place could cause other problems that greatly increased costs and suffering. MS Australia pointed out that for the lack of a pressure mattress, people often ended up spending long periods in hospital because of pressure sores on their skin. Illogicality engendered further inefficiency.

Some state government programs specifically excluded aids for those living in aged care—bad luck for those placed there because no other bed was available.

The committee concluded that a national equipment strategy should be part of the next CSTDA. In the third CSTDA round of funding, in 2001, things improved for parents caring for their children with disability: those aged sixty-five to sixty-nine were entitled to two weeks' respite care a year, when the child would be placed somewhere—anywhere—so the parents could have a break. Those aged seventy and above got four weeks' respite care for their children. That was a system that was not working.

When respite came too late, parents would sometimes abandon their children. The inquiry heard of one case where a sole-parent mother developed breast cancer. She was hospitalised, and entrusted her disabled teen son to her mother. The grandmother told the authorities she could not cope, which resulted in the boy being taken in for respite care. The son was happy in care. On being released from hospital, the mother thought that his being in care was best—she left him there, refusing to collect him. With no other option, the authorities found the boy long-term accommodation.

The very fact that carers needed respite pointed to shortcomings in the services being, or not being, provided, especially regarding accommodation. People who should have been in accommodation were instead ending up in respite beds, further clogging the system.

～

The 2007 Senate report found that while, over time, there had been improvements in transparency, accountability and data collection, it was still the case that measuring the outcomes of the services provided, and gauging the level of unmet needs, was beyond governments' capability.

In the opinion of the Tasmanian government, the CSTDA remained a funding mechanism and nothing more—a government spending machine with no agreed goals, no destination, no defined purpose. Yes, the CSTDA helped, but it was wandering aimlessly in the dark.

Given the lack of data, and the different programs offered by the different states, overall it was impossible to provide uniform and equitable support for people with disability nationwide. Those differences meant also that it was still not possible to have any clear idea of what was needed. The only certain thing was that the system, if 'system' is not too strong a word, was broken.

The Australian National Audit Office (ANAO) stated the problem bluntly: 'There are currently no adequate measures of whether, or to what extent, the CSTDA is meeting its objectives.' Further, the incomparable nature of data collected by the states meant the commonwealth had no way of driving improvement of services.

The same could be said of the quality of services being provided by third parties. Governments had a responsibility to ensure that service providers were in fact providing the services they were being paid for. Easier said than done, even when 'consumers' complained about the quality of service. The ANAO was equally blunt about this: it found the lack of performance benchmarks severely limited the capacity of government to improve the efficiency, effectiveness or quality of services.

On that topic, the Victorian government said in its submission that there were neither incentives nor a framework for pursuing improved outcomes for people receiving services, or for even measuring the outcomes.

The Australian Federation of Disability Organisations put its finger on the problem, arguing that the CSTDA was not a 'co-ordinated high-level policy document'. The whole system was crisis driven, it contended, the result being that short-term interventions took precedence over systemic reforms. Perhaps the main example of this was the provision of accommodation support, which was taking up a larger and larger share of the budget—a recurring theme that was becoming apparent to many in the sector, and to which we shall return.

The Western Australian Disability Coalition had come to the same conclusion. It was of the opinion that the CSTDA's objectives and principles had been watered down in each successive agreement and ultimately had disappeared from view—largely because the system was perpetually responding to crises.

That view was seconded by Victoria's Office of the Public Advocate, which submitted that the vision of a full life for those with disability had become elusive.

Claire Moore agrees. 'It was more about safety than inclusion'—the bar had got so low that if the CSTDA provided accommodation, then its job was done. People with disability were 'separate but safe, there was a great degree of separation. Really, the system was broken. It didn't matter what your needs were, the system was important, and the system would determine who would get support or not. And they just ran out of money.'

The end result, according to the WA Disability Coalition, was 'a very heavy cost to people with disabilities and their families, to government and to the taxpayer'.

The cost, indeed, was great. In 2005–06 the total cost of the CSTDA was $3.5 billion—$1 billion from Canberra, the rest from the states. On top of that was the almost $8 billion for the Disability Support Pension, just over $1 billion for the Carer Allowance and another $1 billion for the Carer Payment. So, $13.5 billion—that $13.5 billion bought an awful lot of misery.

The joint funding arrangements, shared between the commonwealth and the states, were another inherent problem. They allowed blame-shifting at every level. While it was clear in theory that the commonwealth had responsibility for employment services and the states had responsibility for providing other services—accommodation support, community support, community access, respite—the division of responsibility was not always so clear cut in practice. And when anyone complained that a service they needed was not available, the state could always say Canberra had not provided the funds; Canberra could always say in response it had, but the states had not spent them wisely.

Someone receiving personal care and support might have to deal with three or four different agencies, all of which might have different assessment processes. That became even more complicated if the individual concerned had multiple disability needs. To say the administrative burden on the disabled, and their carers, was weighty is an understatement. Having to tell the same story over and over, and then over again, and then again when the relevant staff turned over, was more salt in the already weeping wound. And there was a built-in incentive when telling your story to make it sound as bad as possible—which is demeaning, demoralising and injurious to your pride. This was especially ill suited to people mustering the fortitude to cope with an already difficult situation. And carers complained repeatedly that the time they needed to devote to their loved ones was eaten up by hours spent negotiating the bureaucratic maze—a maze that frequently led to a dead end, with all time spent in it wasted.

The necessity of having to renew applications and repeat your story when the disability was—and was always going to be—permanent was particularly disheartening. This was the point where bureaucracy inflicted pain and suffering: to be asked if your need has passed when there was no chance of recovering from, say, paraplegia was infuriating for those being asked.

Claire Moore says, years later, 'You would have a member of your family with significant disabilities that were never going to get better. You were constantly filling in the forms and then being told "Sorry, we've run out of money, of packages, this year," and people were actually being actively excluded rather than included. The constant evidence we had was from families who talked about the fact that there was no personal understanding. And I think that frustration was just building up to such a level that something had to give. Disability hadn't been a major priority for a long time. It was too hard; too hard and too expensive.'

So, the sorts of questions being asked seemed to signify complete ignorance on behalf of the bureaucracy, which would only make the recipient feel that no one cared, no one understood. 'Why', pleaded one woman in her submission to the inquiry, 'do I have to go on answering these questions?'

The answer was that privacy laws (all the rage at the time) prevented the sharing of people's health information, meaning that the answers you provided last time around could not be accessed again by anyone else in the future. The inquiry suggested applicants should be able to consent to their assessment information being shared.

Applying for help, rather than it being granted on a needs basis, had another consequence: it placed the applicant in competition with every other applicant. Said one submission: 'Family carers are required to portray the needs of their family member with a disability in the worst possible light, as being a burden on them and their family, and I think this has enormous implications. There is a risk of devaluing people with disabilities. I think also it requires an enormous bureaucracy to supervise who gets funding … so providing services on the basis of pitting people's needs against each other consumes resources and has an effect even in terms of simple human dignity.'

Many of those applying had ended up knowing each other because they mixed in the same circles, using the same services. Guilt set in for those who had received funding when they knew people just as deserving who had failed in their applications. On the other side, those who missed out felt envy. Then there was the suspicion. *How much did that other family gild the lily in their application? Has my child missed out because someone else exaggerated? Has my child missed out because I was too proud to properly describe how awful our case is?* It was a terrible situation in which to be trapped—and it gave the lie to any argument about so-called rights. Rights were dependent on arbitrary funds—that was the ignoble reality that anyone negotiating the system would ultimately have to face.

Filling out forms also created difficulties for those with low literacy. The inquiry heard the case of a Vietnamese woman who had a son with severe disabilities, a husband dying of cancer and another son with serious health problems, who was repeatedly denied help. She was incapable of expressing her situation in writing, and culturally disinclined to do so because of an unpreparedness to complain. If the onus had been reversed—and her situation was assessed independently, rather than her having to describe it—she, in all likelihood, would have received the help she needed years earlier.

Resources were meant to be distributed according to need. The ANAO most clearly expressed the problem: the lack of a conceptual model of needs meant 'there is a significant risk that services provided under the CSTDA may not be provided to those recipients in most need across Australia'.

Recognising the injustice, the inquiry recommended the problem be solved by accurate and comprehensive assessments of each individual applicant. It noted that the model in aged care, of multidisciplinary aged care assessment teams meeting applicants face to face, had general support. It said such teams should also advise would-be clients of services available to them, easing their way out of the bureaucratic maze. Further, the teams could assess from the start the more complex needs of those with multiple disabilities. It hoped, too, that making this change could prevent cost-shifting between levels of government, reduce the administrative burden on carers and go at least some way to getting an estimate of unmet needs.

All the problems were exacerbated by the fact that only one commonwealth government department—Families, Community Services and Indigenous Affairs (FaCSIA)—was a party to the CSTDA but as many as seven departments could actually be involved in service provision. Some argued that FaCSIA may have been the lead agency but was the one least involved in actually delivering services.

The much-hoped-for 'whole of government' approach remained a distant ideal.

One suggestion put on the table was the idea of a single department to handle all matters. Failing that, another idea was shifting all responsibility to the commonwealth.

Centralisation also got support from those who baulked at the problem of the states being primarily responsible for funding provision of services while the commonwealth had much more financial capacity at its disposal to do so—the so-called 'vertical fiscal imbalance'. Having the commonwealth completely fund the states would, however, create the problem of one entity spending the money of another entity, which for obvious reasons can easily go awry.

Moving the other way, and having the commonwealth fund and provide the services, would create its own difficulty: the commonwealth had no experience in doing so, while the states did.

There were, in short, more challenges than there were solutions.

∽

The ageing of Australia's population had also reared its head in the national conversation—and it became apparent that this was a huge looming problem in disability.

Aged parents caring for their disabled children emerged as perhaps the biggest problem facing the system, a problem that the committee confronted head on. It concluded that there was no simple, palatable, workable and affordable solution—not within the current framework of thinking.

Demographics clearly demonstrated that the need for workers in aged care, community services and disability would increase precisely at the time that the available pool of workers would decrease—meaning things were only going to get worse. Feeding into all this was the fact that, like the rest of the population, people with disability were living longer, so would spend more time in care.

There were 454 000 people over sixty-five providing care to people with a disability, and about one quarter of those were the primary carer. Many had provided primary care for decades. The toll—emotionally, physically, financially, socially—was immense.

Many of those 454 000 people would soon need aged care themselves. Or be incapable of supporting their loved one. Or die. The agonising question for those carers was 'What happens to my child when I die, or when I can no longer provide care?'

Women did most of the unpaid work. Overwhelmingly, in 68 per cent of cases, the primary carer was the mother. Fathers were the primary carer in 6.5 per cent of cases, just slightly above 6.3 per cent for female relatives other than the mother. Husbands and wives looking after their partner accounted for about 9 per cent of cases. Many carers also had dual-care responsibilities, looking after their ageing parents as well.

In 2005 Carers Australia had commissioned Access Economics to research the contribution of unpaid carers. Access Economics found that about 2.6 million Australians—that's around one in eight— provided 1.2 billion hours of unpaid care annually, representing a hidden cost of $31 billion. When asked to repeat the research in 2010, Access Economics found that the unpaid carers now totalled 2.9 million people, and primary carers 540 000 people, and unpaid hours had increased to 1.32 billion. The hidden cost had leapt to $40 billion. The consequences if these people no longer provided that labour, due to inability, incapacity or death, would be staggering.

Further, the opportunity cost to those providing care who lost out on paid work they otherwise could have done was estimated at $6.5 billion—half a percentage point of gross domestic product (GDP). Which is not merely to say that these people were missing out on work opportunities but that the nation was missing out on their contributions to the economy.

The National Carers Coalition had estimated that the cost of proper accommodation for all Australians with disability would amount to $10.9 billion, an amount big enough to make any treasurer blanch.

The committee's inquiry made the situation clear: the system relied on the unpaid labour of hundreds of thousands of people—mainly women, many of them ageing—who would soon be unable to contribute that labour.

The nation was sitting on a ticking time bomb that would inevitably explode.

These were the big structural problems—but there were myriad others.

There was an issue with informal care that needed addressing: for all the love and attention that family members could give, they did not have the specialist skills of professionals. They could not improve outcomes in the way that, say, physiotherapists or counsellors could.

As well, the trajectory of someone with a lifelong disability could be very different from that of someone with a late-onset disability, resulting in very different needs at different stages of their lives. These complexities again prompted the committee to recognise that tailored services that directly responded to the needs of the individual, as opposed to generic groups, were necessary if the services were to live up to their rhetoric.

Indexation was another concern. In order to provide the same level of service, funds have to be increased just to keep up with inflation. But Commonwealth departments had to cut spending each year—the so-called 'efficiency dividend', which was usually care of automation and the increased use of technology. The inquiry heard that the efficiency dividend was not appropriate in the disability sector, where wages were the greatest component of costs, and where savings from automation and technology were rarely available.

The West Australian government pointed to a structural problem: meeting urgent needs always came at the cost of things like early intervention, which had the capacity to bring down long-term costs while improving outcomes at the same time. It's the simple fact of maintenance: delaying action will just defer a cost until it becomes bigger, and the situation worse.

Early diagnosis and early intervention in the area of disability were severely lacking—and these were the things that gave the biggest benefits, especially for children with autism. Early treatment could minimise the disability. Yet, there was a waiting list of two years even to get a diagnosis of autism.

Education was another common area of criticism. People complained about schools turning away their children; and that when they were admitted, they were not being properly taught. It was a problem McLucas knew all too well. Before becoming a senator, she was a primary school teacher, beginning that career just at the time Queensland was mainstreaming education of children with disability.

'Philosophically, we knew mainstreaming was the right thing to do—special schools were not the answer. But there was no extra resourcing or support ... I don't think I was given training in regard to disability. So I was actually quite worried that I was not skilled up enough to support children with disabilities. I think I was halfway through my career as a teacher before I knew what "autism" meant.'

The inquiry also showed that one of the problems with the existing data collection, which was very incomplete, was that it did not measure outcomes. More than one submission pointed out that reporting a certain number of people received service A or service B told nothing about how effective those services were.

Every part of the sector could recount multiple stories of people receiving no access, or inadequate access, to the service they needed. It had been noted during the late 1990s, when Canberra topped up funding under the second CSTDA by $150 million, to cover its last two years. The states were to match it—they ended up doubling it. The Commonwealth did the same again in the next five-year funding batch—but noted that the information provided by the states was not good enough to form a picture of what was actually needed.

Looming perhaps most dangerously, however, was an iceberg that could up-end the whole system: unmet need. It was an iceberg because no one knew exactly how big it was. One thing was clear, though: it was very, very big.

AIHW had been trying its best to quantify unmet need for some years. As far back as 1996, it calculated there were 13 400 people who needed more in the way of accommodation support and respite services, and 12 000 people needing day programs—always, it said, erring on the conservative side with its figures.

Some states did not keep lists of those awaiting services. Victoria did, and it reported that 4500 people were waiting for accommodation and community support, as well as a 76 per cent increase in those on the urgent list for supported accommodation. Of those, one in six were being cared for by a family member aged seventy-five or more. That is crisis territory.

In South Australia, 2200 people with intellectual disabilities were on an urgent list for accommodation. When you consider that the cost of someone with disability living in a share house was about $93 000 a year, and the cost of someone living in an institution was about $82 000 a year, the funding shortfall was going to be in the hundreds of millions, for sure—maybe in the billions.

Reporting again, in 2001, AIHW found that more than 5000 carers needing respite had received none, having been left to care for their dependents without help. The figures were alarming—and did not include under-met needs, or needs that were met inappropriately, or the needs of people who had given up and no longer interacted.

One submission, by a young man living with cerebral palsy, showed how someone could be receiving services but whose needs fall a long way short of being met. Patrick lived by himself in a unit designed for people with disability. He wanted to live with others, preferably those in a condition similar to his, but no such accommodation was available. So he was living a life of social isolation.

'First and foremost, the level of unmet need is largely unknown,' the committee concluded, 'and pressures within the system, including an ageing population, will result in an ever increasing demand for services.'

All the relevant parties continued to uphold the mantra that people with disability had rights, including the right to lead a full life, as similar

as possible to the rest of society; yet, at the same time, everyone recognised that the funding to help deliver that type of life was not there. For
the moment, the only way out of that intellectual impasse was cognitive
dissonance: simultaneously maintaining two propositions that contra-
dicted each other.

The further problem was a deep structural one: again, the funding
model of a finite bucket of money, no matter how large, was fundamentally at odds with the notion of rights. You simply could not say a disabled
person had a right to anything if that right was extinguished at the
arbitrary moment that funding was exhausted. That moment was by
definition arbitrary, if the allocation of funds was made in ignorance of
the needs to be met. And here another fundamental contradiction arose:
budgets are rigid, not elastic. Open-ended expenditure is at odds with
finite allocations. Budgets require a dollar sign, not an infinity symbol.

⌐

Lastly, the committee turned to alternative funding models.

It considered reversing the position of the service receiver: one proposal was that, instead of them receiving a service, turning that person
into an employer, as it were, by funding them directly, and letting them
choose which services they wanted, and which provider they wanted
them from. The argument was that, as things stood, governments were,
in effect, providing financial support to service providers, not to people
with disability.

The Australian Federation of Disability Organisations submitted that the bureaucratic model in place was inflexible and restrictive,
not allowing people with disability to make choices and take risks,
and removing their agency by limiting the decisions they could make.
Reversing the relationship would empower the recipient, letting them
choose which services they needed and when. It could, in theory, lead

to lower administrative costs, and the economic theory of the day (and today) posited that increased competition to provide services would drive down their prices while increasing their quality. Such a change could turn a closed market into an open and competitive one.

The other side of the coin was also considered—would such arrangements add even more complexity to a system already difficult to negotiate; would they add to the already heavy administrative burden on recipients and their carers; would they lead to more isolation by removing case managers; would service brokers simply end up replacing case managers, and add another layer of cost; would government be able to simply wash its hands and walk away once payments were made? The committee chose not to make a decision on reversing the position of the service receiver, saying it needed more information on likely costs and benefits.

Even in that area, a new problem had emerged. Families were now legally liable for injuries suffered by those who visited their homes, which were now, practically speaking, their workplaces. The National Carers Coalition commented: 'What is becoming more and more apparent is that this industry of "paid help in the home" is not only an ever increasing encroachment upon the privacy of the family home, but it has now declared the family home to be a "workplace". This declared workplace is now a place in which families are being sued as "third party liable" under WorkCover regulations in some if not all states. Laws which protect paid care workers but give no protection to the caring family are an abomination that will see more and more families think twice before having any in-home help for which they can be potentially sued.' The notion that the carer family of a disabled person was legally liable for any injury sustained by a visiting service provider was a cruel joke—except it wasn't a joke, it was a real and serious legal problem.

Two submissions provided a big idea for the funding model.

A big idea that could give a way out.

A national compensation scheme.

The committee noted that other countries already operated such schemes. In 1995 Germany had instituted just such a scheme that provided long-term care insurance, was comprehensive and mandatory, and covered 88 per cent of the population. As well as providing both at-home and institutional care, it provided cash payments to family caregivers.

Japan had overhauled its system in 2000, bringing in a scheme that covered 90 per cent of all costs, be they at home or in institutions, funded through the tax system.

New Zealand, too, the inquiry noted briefly, had a national no-fault scheme covering accidents, which had been running since the early 1970s.

Attention was also given to similar but restricted schemes in Australia, such as Victoria's Transport Accident Commission scheme, which provided aid to those injured in car accidents, irrespective of fault—meaning that it did not matter if the injured party, the other party, or anyone or anything was at fault. That was in contrast to the common law, where there was no case unless someone was at fault. The only thing that mattered was injury, which automatically generated compensation. That system was open-ended: recipients could rest assured their aid would not be withdrawn randomly depending on funding.

The Young People in Nursing Homes National Alliance made a startling submission.

First, it painted a picture. The people it represented were doubly disadvantaged, being unable by law to access state-based services while being housed in Commonwealth-funded facilities. These young people—there were 7000 of them in nursing homes at the time, taking up 5 per cent of aged care beds, where they were condemned to live the rest of their lives exclusively in the company of the aged—were denied services available to others. They were also not counted in those awaiting services—that is, in the unmet need tally—under the CSTDA. But, the submission continued, simply taking these people from aged care facilities into the general disability system was not an option, because the services they required did not exist. Without reform, the problem would only continue to grow.

The alliance submitted: 'we believe that something like a social insurance levy, similar to the Medicare levy in intent and scope, is needed for long-term care and support'. It pointed out that building up funds by ongoing contributions would create the necessary reserve balance when more services were needed as the population aged.

In October 2007, just a month before the federal election, Bronwyn Morkham's Young People in Nursing Homes National Alliance ran a summit. It called for all states to run a no-fault accident scheme like Victoria's, for all accidents, not just car accidents—and that this scheme then be extended to cover catastrophic disability.

That is, in essence, the idea of the National Disability Insurance Scheme.

'Our alliance was formed in 2002 and we had been pushing this idea since 2003,' Bronwyn Morkham explains all these years later. 'We convened a conference in 2003 and ran a stream on the idea of a social insurance scheme.' The alliance had examined the New Zealand scheme, run by its Accident Compensation Corporation, and brought a participant over from NZ. 'We looked at the compensation schemes, like the TAC in Victoria, and we thought the principles they espoused should be transferred to disability. We were after a catastrophic injury scheme to start with. We thought it was better to start with an injury scheme, mainly because we had the compensation schemes in place and they could show how it was done—their processes and procedures were in place.'

Disability advocate Raelene West made a similar submission. She pointed out that disability services were, in different states, funded by between four and eight different bodies, once you counted those covered by WorkCover, car accident insurance schemes and Veterans' Affairs (not to mention those covered by common law negligence cases). This funding further distorted the true cost of disability.

Ms West also recommended a national insurance scheme, directing the committee's attention to New Zealand's system, as a working model of a comprehensive, national scheme, one capable of subsuming schemes already in place. As well as the great benefit of providing universal coverage, Ms West argued, only via such a national scheme could the system become sustainable and its in-built inequities be removed.

The Victorian government submitted that its car accident compensation scheme could be expanded nationally and could be enlarged to include catastrophic injuries beyond those incurred in car accidents— and, further, that it would consider going it alone if there was no impetus for a national scheme.

MS Australia took the logic of all this one step further in its submission: what was needed was an actuarial approach, to generate knowledge of needs into the future and start planning for that, rather than going from crisis to crisis.

But one thing was clear: the gap between need and services provided was growing. Funding, even though it was increasing, was falling further and further behind.

The committee recommended researching 'the issues encountered in the introduction of alternative funding overseas'.

෨

The committee's report made the problems clear.

Deinsitutionalisation had failed.

Accommodation needs were not being met.

Support for people with disability was too often not available.

Aids for people with disability were too often not available.

The cost of accommodation would explode in the coming years, as ageing carers could no longer cope.

The cost of support labour would also explode.

The extra costs would eventually be in the tens of billions of dollars.

The system was a mess, unnavigable and indecipherable, making people's lives a misery.

People with disability were being failed miserably. As were their families, who bore the brunt. The nation was missing out on what both people with disability and their families had to offer.

The system was being driven by crises, to the point that it, too, was in crisis.

The Senate report came to a resounding conclusion: 'To ensure a coordinated national approach to improving the delivery of disability services, to ensure that people access the services they require throughout their lives … and to ensure that future need for services is adequately addressed, a renewed national strategic approach is required. The Committee considers that a national disability strategy would reaffirm our commitment to equity and inclusiveness in Australian society for people with disability.'

A total rethink was necessary, and it needed to be national, not state-based, with a strategy 'designed to address the complexity of needs of people with disability and their carers in all aspects of their lives'. Labor promised such a strategy in the 2007 election campaign. Victory in that election meant these problems were now Labor's.

Bill Shorten would inherit them as the parliamentary secretary for disability services. His senior minister would be Jenny Macklin, who had years—decades, even—of experience in social policy.

Macklin was fully aware of the extent of the problem. 'When we came into government in 2007, this much was known, that there was significant unmet need for support for people with disabilities. Internationally, we came close to the bottom of the table among the member nations of the OECD when it came to the amount that we spent on disability services. So, consequently, life was a terrible lottery for people with disability in Australia. Here in Victoria, if you acquired a disability in an accident caused by a car, a motorcycle, bus, tram or train, you were automatically covered by the Transport Accident Commission's no-fault insurance scheme. But if you acquired a disability in any other way, you were pretty much on your own. Not only that, but the costs of disability were also escalating as people live longer and aged-parent carers were no longer able to cope. In other words, Australia was paying more and more to prop up a broken system.'

Shorten was new to the scene. He had little to no knowledge or experience of disability. He did not know what to expect. What he found disturbed and shocked him.

'I feel like I'd found this hidden city in our midst,' he says now. 'You know when explorers go looking for cities in the jungle? We had a city in our midst in which people were living behind walls. We had people in exile in our own cities and suburbs. I hadn't seen such chronic and entrenched disability in my life. Millions of our fellow Australians were living in exile; it was like there was an invisible wall around them. The rest couldn't see them and they weren't getting the same opportunity as everybody else.'

TO THE SUMMIT

———

KEVIN RUDD'S GOVERNMENT came to power on 24 November 2007—and barely took time out for an Iced VoVo before getting down to business.

Rudd had promised that he would make an apology to Aboriginal Australia—in particular, to the Stolen Generations—as a matter of priority.

The forty-second Parliament of Australia was inaugurated like no other before it: with a Welcome to Country. Ngambri elder Matilda House, draped in a possum cloak, told the assembled audience in the Members Hall that 'for thousands of years, our people have observed this protocol. It is a good and honest and a decent and human act to reach out and make sure everyone has a place and is welcome.' Message sticks were exchanged and a smoking ceremony enacted. Dancers, both traditional and contemporary, performed, their job made more difficult by the rain that seeped through the roof onto the marble floor.

The weather the next day, Wednesday 13 February 2008, was much more agreeable; no bad thing for the thousands who had come to Canberra and converged on Parliament House, keen to watch and listen to proceedings on giant screens in the surrounding grounds. When the parliament sat for the first time, Prime Minister Rudd stood and moved the first motion.

He then delivered the long-awaited Apology to Australia's Indigenous people—long awaited, as it had been urged by *Bringing Them Home* a decade earlier. That report had laid out the awful details of how, for generations, Aboriginal Australians had been forcibly taken from their families as a matter of government policy, both state and federal, the latter by virtue of events in the Northern Territory.

Within four years of that urging, all the state governments had apologised. Hundreds of thousands of Australians had taken responsibility themselves and made their own apology, marching on Sorry Day from its inception in 1998, particularly in 2000, when more than a quarter of a million marched across Sydney Harbour Bridge. Hundreds of thousands more signed their names in Sorry Books.

When Rudd stood and addressed the parliament, he did what his predecessor, Liberal leader John Howard, had refused to do for the past decade. Howard, however, was not a sitting member of this parliament. The people of Bennelong—the seat straddling Sydney's north shore and western suburbs, named after the first Indigenous Australian to be forcibly separated from his family—had decided he would no longer represent them.

'The time has now come for the nation to turn a new page in Australia's history,' Rudd began, 'by righting the wrongs of the past and so moving forward with confidence to the future. We apologise for the laws and policies of successive Parliaments and governments that have inflicted profound grief, suffering and loss on these our fellow Australians. We apologise especially for the removal of Aboriginal and Torres Strait Islander children from their families, their communities and their country.'

The words 'apologise' and 'sorry' were a steady refrain throughout, clear and unambiguous. Sorry for the pain and suffering, sorry for the mothers and fathers, sisters and brothers, cousins, uncles and aunties torn apart from each other, sorry for the indignity, sorry for the degradation.

Outside parliament, the hushed silence of the gathered crowd was broken only by stifled sobbing, from the men and women, young and old, black and white, who listened respectfully, as First Australians heard the words they had waited so long to hear. The scene was repeated across the country. Schools stopped to watch, as did myriad workplaces—factories, offices, newsrooms—and places of entertainment—cafes and pubs. People gathered far and wide in public spaces where more big screens had been set up, and in private homes, where people watched on their own big screens. In the House, Jenny Macklin, the minister for Indigenous affairs, kept herself from crying—Macklin was well known for letting the tears flow as they may.

The sobs turned to tears when Rudd changed gear to tell the story of Nanna Nungala Fejo, 'as she prefers to be called', who was born in the late 1920s. No one at the time bothered to keep accurate records of the births and deaths of Indigenous people. No need—they weren't considered part of the population, and wouldn't be until the nation voted otherwise in the 1967 referendum.

Nanna Nungala Fejo could remember her time in the camps outside Tennant Creek in the Northern Territory, singing and dancing around the campfire. She could remember, too, the day the 'welfare men' came; a day for which her parents had prepared, digging holes in the creek bank in which the children could hide. On that day, it was to no avail. 'The kids were found,' Rudd continued. 'They ran for their mothers, screaming, but they could not get away. They were herded and piled onto the back of the truck. Tears flowing, her mum tried clinging to the sides of the truck as her children were taken away to the Bungalow in Alice [Springs], all in the name of protection.'

Nanna Nungala Fejo was taken with her sister, brother and cousin. Her family was then broken once more—her brother and cousin were sent to different missions. The children never saw their mother again— she died a broken, bereft woman.

In the lead-up to the Apology, Rudd was writing his speech at the prime ministerial residence in Canberra, the Lodge. He was writing and drafting, rewriting and redrafting—and he knew something was missing. He knew he had to talk to someone who knew more than he did; someone who had lived it. He found someone: he went and listened to Nanna Nungala Fejo as she told him her story.

'I asked Nanna Fejo what she would have me say today about her story. She thought for a few moments then said that what I should say today was that all mothers are important. And she added: "Families— keeping them together is very important. It's a good thing that you are surrounded by love and that love is passed down the generations. That's what gives you happiness."'

When Kevin Rudd sat listening to Nanna Fejo, he did so in the company of Jenny Macklin. 'Imagine what it is like for the PM to sit in somebody's sitting room for a couple of hours on a Saturday morning with her family sitting around her—her little grandchild, three months old in her mother's arms,' Macklin said later. Rudd had arrived bearing a present—a bag of oranges, which he had been informed were a favourite of Nanna Fejo. In return, he got his Iced VoVo, as referenced in his election-night victory speech.

Nanna Fejo was at Parliament House that historic day. She wore a T-shirt bearing the word *Thanks*. 'We waited a long time for this,' she told reporters. 'We never thought we would live to see this happen.'

When Rudd's speech ended after half an hour, the packed gallery and the members of parliament—on both sides, excepting those who boycotted—rose to applaud. It showed the truth in the maxim of former prime minister Paul Keating: when you change the prime minister, you change the country.

The country had, indeed, just changed—it was time to listen. It was time to tell the truth. It was time for the disenfranchised to be awarded their rights.

Truth is a powerful thing. It always wins in the end. A politician forgets this at their peril.

Hard as it may be to believe, Macklin had another meeting that afternoon whose import was just as great, if not more—about a class of people just as neglected, marginalised and oppressed.

～

That first day of the new parliament was not the first time Jenny Macklin had witnessed tears being shed over the Apology.

Weeks earlier, on 11 December, she had launched *Us Taken-Away Kids* at Sydney's Old Customs House, a book that gathered the stories of stolen First Nations people, issued to commemorate the ten-year anniversary of *Bringing Them Home*. She had mentioned to some of those at the event that there would, indeed, be an apology from the prime minister—that news itself had been enough to bring forth tears.

Events as momentous as Kevin Rudd's Apology don't just happen. Macklin was on the job, gathering advice on what should be said, and how, and to whom. Born in Brisbane in 1953, Macklin graduated from the University of Melbourne with an honours degree in commerce. She had been associated with the Labor Party in one form or another since the 1970s; for the past eleven years, as the sitting member for the seat of Jagajaga, which takes in the hilly north-eastern Melbourne suburbs that skirt the banks of the Yarra River. The seat, perhaps unfortunately, is named for three brothers of the Wurundjeri clan. They supposedly were among those who signed a contract with the bushranger-hunting, Aboriginal-massacring and child-stealing syphilitic publican John Batman, exchanging 240 000 hectares of their ancestral land around Melbourne and Geelong for a bunch of tomahawks, blankets, scissors, flour and the like. William Buckley, the escaped convict who lived with Indigenous Australians for thirty-two years, immediately saw through the supposed deal as self-evidently preposterous, knowing that these people would not have made it. Land, quite simply, was not for sale.

In Sydney, Governor Richard Bourke took an equally dim view of the transaction, but for rather different reasons—as far as he and the law were concerned, the Crown of Great Britain owned *all* the land of Australia, and only it could sell it. For all that, Batman appears to have been about the only white man to offer any payment for land.

Until now, Macklin's years in parliament had been spent in opposition. For the past twelve months, she had been the shadow minister for Indigenous affairs and reconciliation. Now she was the minister. That, however, was not the extent of her ministry: her portfolio also made her the minister for families, housing and community services, a shadow post she had held since entering parliament.

It was in that capacity that a week before the *Us Taken-Away Kids* launch, on 3 December, not two weeks after the election, she had attended the National Disability Awards in Canberra, honouring outstanding individual achievement. It was a gala event for the sector— think Brownlow or Dally M Medal—with everyone who could make it in attendance.

Macklin was accompanied by Bill Shorten, another Victorian Labor MP, newly elected to the inner north-west Melbourne seat of Maribyrnong, also an Indigenous word, whose meaning is a matter of dispute. Only that day, Shorten had been formally appointed parliamentary secretary for disabilities and children's services. Those who keep a close eye on who gets what when positions of power are distributed in the nation's capital thought Shorten might have been short-changed; the forty-year-old was the Victorian state Labor president, and had been state and national head of the Australian Workers' Union. What was exercising their thinking more, perhaps, was Shorten's outsize profile for someone who was still finding his way around Parliament House. For he had shot to prominence the previous year, appearing daily in the wall-to-wall media coverage at the site of the Beaconsfield gold mine disaster in Tasmania. The mine had collapsed on Anzac Day. Fourteen escaped that day; one, Larry Knight, died. Two others, Brant Webb and Todd Russell, were trapped underground, where they would remain for two weeks until they were brought safely to the surface.

Shorten was dazed by the appointment—'the first twenty-four hours I didn't know what I'd got'. Given his union background and experience on the board of AustralianSuper, he had thought he was likely to be appointed to industrial relations or finance. He had no experience or knowledge of disability, nor of children's services—'I didn't even have a kid.'

If the Rudd government had hit the ground running, no one was moving faster than Macklin and Shorten.

Nicole Lawder, CEO of the Deafness Forum of Australia, was one of those in attendance at the awards that Canberra summer evening, with representatives of a newborn government still aglow with the flush of victory.

'Jenny Macklin and Bill Shorten turned up beaming from ear to ear, saying "Have we got good news for you!" So, that's where it all started, if you like. Not long after that I was in Parliament House, at a function … about deafness. I was walking back through the foyer of Parliament House and there's Bill Shorten coming in the opposite direction and he sort of said, "Oh, hi, I've asked for you to join a ministerial council on disability, you'll hear about it shortly." And I went, "Oh yeah, sure." Thinking, you just say that, but anyway, I did get this invitation to join the committee and off it went.'

It wasn't apparent to Lawder, or perhaps anyone else, exactly what was happening. Nor how big it was. Or that it would change the nation as deeply and indelibly as the Apology.

'I was appointed parliamentary secretary and was not really sure where to begin,' Shorten recalls years later, 'so I went back to my approach from my union days and decided that I'd consult with as many people as possible.'

The first thing Shorten did was have a chat with his mentor, Bill Kelty, the former head of the Australian Council of Trade Unions (ACTU), who sat on the board of the Reserve Bank and was the man behind the Accord—something much in vogue at the time. Their relationship went back to when Shorten was still a lawyer, when Kelty advised him that the best apprenticeship for politics was in the union movement. Kelty said to him now, 'Bill, this could be the making of you.' His advice was to do what he did in the union: organise. 'There were good people in disability, good people,' Kelty recalls, 'but they didn't know how to organise. Didn't know how to negotiate. So that's why they never got what they wanted. I said to him, "This is like your union days. You have to organise. And campaign." So Bill corralled them. Got them all into one group. Got them to agree. Made sure there was no dissent. Then they campaigned.'

Shorten also consulted Julia Gillard, the deputy prime minister. Her advice was that this 'was an opportunity to develop new skills and show another side of himself'.

All of which is very much how Shorten describes events.

'So I set off around the country, talking to individuals and families of people with disabilities,' he says. 'I was gobsmacked at the lack of services, especially in non-metro areas. I was talking to people with disabilities a lot and their carers, and they were all telling me that it was the system that was broken, and I started to imagine how that idea could get promoted. That's when I decided that we needed to build a coalition.'

Building bridges, binding groups, uniting people—it is a greater political art than dividing them. It is also much harder and takes a lot longer.

The day after Shorten's appointment, he was back in Melbourne, where he had a meeting with Bronwyn Morkham from the Young

People in Nursing Homes National Alliance. 'I will never forget it,' says Morkham. 'We sat in the Carnegie library. I started to talk to him about a social insurance scheme. With many people you have to cycle through this twice. I did it once and I was about to come back to it again, and he stopped me and said, "You don't need to tell me twice, Bronwyn, I got that." So, Bill picked it up—he was eager to make his mark, and rightly so.'

Having realised that what he needed to do was listen, to understand people's experience of the disability system and of the difficulties encountered when tackling the maze of services that might or not might be available, Shorten soon made the imaginative leap that this was what the government and the nation needed to do too. First, he created the body that government would have to listen to, a body that would advise it on all things disability.

'So, I set up the ministerial council—the National People with Disabilities and Carer Council [NPDCC]. What I did was not just get the usual suspects: I got a broader coalition of people. I got union leaders, business leaders, some who had disabilities, others who had family disabilities, just to widen the debate.'

The council soon had a chair, Rhonda Galbally, who was well versed in the field, having worked in and around government, business and the disability sector since the 1980s, when she was a senior policy officer for the Victorian Council of Social Service. In addition to her aforementioned work, she had been instrumental at VicHealth in establishing the Health Promotion Foundation, which was funded in advance by a 5 per cent state levy on tobacco—and had then set out to try to reduce the use of said substance. Galbally was a grand organiser, used to working on things from the ground up, having been the founding CEO of the Australian Commission for the Future, the Australian International Health Institute and the Australian National Preventative Health Agency. She had also been chair of the Royal Women's Hospital.

She now jokes that she was 'chair of the largest government council in Australia I had ever seen, much less chaired—twenty-eight members strong, and it had the longest name ever too'.

There was a reason for the long name—any organising body in the field had to look after the concerns of both those with disability and their carers. And, for that matter, the service providers too—but their feelings weren't as important, or as heated, as those of the other two groups.

There was also a reason for so many people being on the council—Shorten was making them talk to each other, which, as we shall see, they had not always done. He also insisted—against strong advice from others—that the body include people from outside the disability sector. While they came from outside the sector, many had experience of disability. That would have consequences: it would spread the message far and wide, into distant networks.

Galbally was against the idea of such a large membership of the council. 'Bill Shorten came to see me very early on. He was responsible for the huge membership of our ministerial council. When he was pushing for this much wider representation, I thought it should just be people with disabilities, and carers. But he was talking mobilisation. He said clearly, you won't get anywhere unless you come together as a sector and then mobilise with the business sector and union movement. I couldn't believe how big the council was, but it was very exciting and rich with ideas and wisdom. A huge success. Bill was absolutely right in broadening it beyond people with disabilities and not worrying about the size, and I was wrong.'

Bill Shorten smiles when reminded of the size of his council. 'Why have a small council when you can have a big one?' he says.

～

Canberra airport is usually busy on a Thursday as politicians, their staff, public servants, lobbyists, journalists and so on get out of town, back to wherever they think is home. Thursday 17 April 2008 was even more busy than usual—but the travellers were headed in the opposite direction. One thousand and two delegates were arriving from all points of the country, ready to play their role in the 2020 summit. The summit had been conceptualised in the very early days of Rudd's prime ministership, announced in the first week of February and given a deadline of twelve weeks' hence, with a promise to report back within a year—it was all happening at breakneck speed. If the Apology had brought fresh air into the national conversation, the summit was a fresh wind, raising spirits, engendering widespread feelings of positivity, as Australians from far and wide were welcomed to contribute ideas for the future of their country.

The delegates were arriving in peak autumn, as the bush capital luxuriated under cloudless blue skies and the air began to cool, fresh but not yet burdened by winter's bitter chill. Having been greeted at the airport, the delegates were treated to a little bit of Canberra, maybe taking in the vivid red, yellow and orange hues of the American elms peppering the suburb of Griffith, or maybe the red poplars and reddish-brown oak trees around Lake Burley Griffin. A little bit of tourism done, the delegates would check in to their hotels before proceeding to dinner. They weren't exactly being duchessed—all the participants were there at their own expense, paying for their own transport and accommodation. They were devoting their time to argument, to debate, to the contest of ideas, all bringing their own vision of where Australia needed to be come 2020. Thursday night would start with dinner, even if it was a working dinner.

For the big names, and some not-so-big names, their entrée was at the Lodge. The delegates taking part in the economics stream, one of ten such streams to which delegates were assigned, would dine at treasury. Those in town to discuss the arts were off to the National Museum.

The naïve view was that the summit would bring forth grand ideas—but of course the summiteers were in town precisely because they *already* had ideas. For many, work had begun long before they arrived in Canberra. Anyone who had thought through the scenario with any degree of precision—a hundred people in each of the ten streams, all fighting for their ideas to dominate, then competing against the other streams, who all had their own big ideas—would have realised that a little caucusing, a little networking, a little strategising beforehand would give their idea the best chance of survival. Anyone who had watched an episode of *Survivor* knew that much, let alone the delegates, who among them had a wealth of experience of getting things done, be it in business, in unions, in government, in the welfare sector—you name it.

As much was admitted several days beforehand by the mastermind who had put the whole shebang together: Glyn Davis, the big-brained vice-chancellor of the University of Melbourne at the time, handpicked by Rudd for his organisational prowess and capacity for ideas. Davis's speciality was public policy and political science, and had combined an outstanding academic career with hands-on public service work, having been director-general of the department of premier and cabinet for Queensland Labor premier Wayne Goss—whose chief of staff had been one Kevin Rudd—and then Peter Beattie.

In the first weeks of his term, Rudd had invited Davis to the Lodge, where he outlined his idea. Not overly enthused by the public service and the ideas it had on the drawing board, Rudd wanted to enlarge the conversation by inviting the general population to take part. The two strolled in the pleasantly modest Lodge gardens as the prime minister put forth his notion, saying that the government had the opportunity to do this just once, and it had to be early in its term. He had drawn the basic outline—ten streams of discussion, further broken down into smaller groups and smaller questions. A week later, Davis was back in Canberra, announcing the summit.

'There is a huge amount of pre-work that has gone on,' he told veteran Canberra journalist Katharine Murphy on the summit's eve. 'We've had pep talks, many of us have already met at state level, some of the groups have already met in small or large groups.' The ground rules—respect and courtesy in discussion—had been made clear to those attending.

Talking to the ABC that same day, Davis showed admirable restraint when asked about the opposition claim that participants would get on average thirty seconds to air their ideas. It seems someone had divided the number of participants by the amount of time for discussions, without consulting an agenda that showed the delegates would be in groups. Anyway, Davis drily noted, 'there's also virtue in listening'.

Davis made it clear that the listening was the first thing government had to do. 'I think it's only reasonable in any rational policy process that you get an opportunity to now hear the other point of view, to hear why, to ask why haven't we done this if it's such an obviously good idea?' Indeed.

It was Davis, along with ten other members of the summit's steering committee, who had chosen the 1002 delegates, determined that they would not be representing specific bodies or interest groups, but speaking as individuals. Davis had set things in place, gathering the forty facilitators, drawn from major consulting firms and working for free, who would shepherd debate; he had commandeered the 'scribes', who would notate the discussions; he had seen to it that the discussions would be recorded and taped. These people, too, were contributing their labour without pay.

All of which spoke to how seriously the whole event was being taken, even if many—in the public, the media, even in government—pooh-poohed the whole thing. Shorten says now it was all a bit like *Utopia*, the biting TV series that mocks the processes of government.

Expectations were high, yet there could not but be misgivings, given the inherently political nature of proceedings—the more experienced attendees would be wary of pre-existing agendas, fearful that they were being used as a prop to validate preordained outcomes. If delegates had not themselves already formed the notion that there would soon be a tsunami of ideas, they would have been aware of it when they were given the 8713 submissions from the general population that had already arrived. Local summits had been held across the nation, resulting in 3000 ideas being submitted to the summit's website. Further submissions could be made after the summit. There had already been a Jewish summit in Sydney because the main event coincided with Passover, precluding many from attending. There had been an African symposium in Melbourne. Summits at primary and secondary schools had been held over three weeks in March. The official summit blog had been live for a week—and many delegates had been active on it, airing ideas and flushing out supporters. There had already been a youth summit in Canberra.

The delegates were all aware that the summit was the brainchild of Rudd, who naturally wanted the event to succeed and to share in its glory. The precedent was clear to everyone—twenty-four years earlier, in April 1983, the freshly elected Hawke government convened the National Economic Summit, at which business joined the ACTU, which had already signed up to the Accord. The Accord, in which unions agreed to wage restraint in return for social and economic benefits, cleared the path for the neoliberal economic reforms enacted over the thirteen years of that government. The model was consensus, of unions and business cooperating rather than fighting, in order to share larger portions of a bigger pie.

Rudd, like his predecessor, wanted to generate a spirit of cooperation, which can do wonders for a government. There was risk involved—and the risk here was of setting expectations too high. If every delegate brought only one idea, that still amounted to a thousand ideas, which was more than any government can handle. Even Mao Zedong had asked for but 100 flowers to bloom—the 'thousand flowers' commonly cited is a misquotation. The proper quote is: 'Letting a hundred flowers blossom and a hundred schools of thought contend is the policy for promoting progress in the arts and the sciences and a flourishing socialist culture in our land.' With the exception of the concluding phrase, the dictum applied well to Rudd's summit. It must be pointed out, however, that if the 2020 summiteers were to be disappointed, they would not be as disappointed as Mao's florists—many of those who took up his invitation to criticise the Communist Party during the Hundred Flowers campaign of 1956–57 were persecuted, sacked, imprisoned and, yes, executed, in the years to follow. There have been no reports of 2020 summiteers being disappeared.

Such dismal thoughts were far from anyone's mind as proceedings got underway that Friday. Rudd repeated his mantra—that government did not have a monopoly on wisdom, and he wanted to hear what the Australian people had to offer.

Beginning, as had his parliament, with an acknowledgement of First Nations people, he declared: 'Today we are trying to do something new. What we are looking for from this Summit are new ideas for our nation's future.'

His rhetoric was biblical—'I have a simple view, which is that without a vision the people do perish' was straight from Proverbs.

One thing in particular stood out among the directions given to delegates—do not let your ideas be constrained by preconceptions of what is possible. Don't worry about cost. Don't worry about size. Don't worry about feasibility. Just give us your ideas; your best ideas.

Expectations were off the charts, which guarantees disappointment, especially if you were listening carefully to Rudd's opening address: he hoped that 'the next two days bring forth, say, a dozen new ideas about how we can shape our nation's future, together'. A dozen?

And so, to business, as the attendees set to work.

The delegates were hived off into their designated streams, to discuss, plan and dream what Australia should look like in 2020, under ten different headings: productivity; economy, sustainability and climate change; rural Australia; health and ageing; Indigenous Australia;

creative Australia; governance; security; and the one that will occupy us here—communities and families.

Each of the streams had been appointed two co-chairs. The Communities stream had Tim Costello and Labor MP Tanya Plibersek, with Hal Bisset as lead facilitator.

Tim Costello was a forceful but engaging man in his early fifties. Educated in Melbourne, he qualified as a lawyer, then studied theology in Switzerland, being ordained as a Baptist minister in 1987, aged thirty-two. A campaigner against the negative effects of alcohol and gambling, he rose to national prominence when he became head of World Vision, especially due to his fundraising of more than $100 million in response to 2004's Boxing Day tsunami.

Plibersek was minister for housing and for the status of women, having been in parliament since 1998. A highly intelligent woman with an easy if firm manner, Plibersek is the child of Slovenian migrants who followed circuitous paths to Australia in the great wave of post–World War II migration.

Hal Bisset's field of expertise, in which he had extensive experience, was the development of affordable housing.

After introductory addresses by Plibersek—who noted the historic opportunity of the occasion and urged participants to think big— and Costello—who focused his attention more narrowly on specific measures to alleviate alcohol's harm, such as volumetric taxation—the delegates in the Community stream were divided into a further ten groups and given three key questions to discuss:

What are the key characteristics of Australia in 2020 that support communities, families, social inclusion?

What are the key challenges we face in reaching these goals by 2020?

What are the key questions we need to ask?

The fact that one of the questions was to ask what questions needed to be asked looks, at first blush, like an absurdity; from another perspective, it acknowledges that ideas might best emerge from the floor.

Post discussion, the delegates reconvened to report. From that, the assigned scribes identified six themes emerging. (The 'scribes' were public servants; also, of course, working for free, which seems like cruel and unusual punishment for not having come up with a thousand policy ideas in the first place.) Groups were reconfigured to discuss these six themes and to report back to the group at large. Those six themes were refined further to four, which were reported to the delegates from other streams when everyone was reunited at the closing session.

The delegates not being short of ideas, the scribes recorded 200 of them. The group was asked to do some editing and come up with four big ideas.

The group that discussed Theme 1, Responding to Disadvantage, reported back with twenty-eight ideas. One of them was: 'Create a National Disability Insurance Scheme, similar to a superannuation scheme, to support the families of people with brain injury from birth or from non-insured accidents'.

Putting to one side the conceptual confusion—an insurance scheme and superannuation are two different things, even if they are vaguely similar—the important point is that the NDIS was now on the agenda. Remarkably, it was there under the name by which it is still known. Names are important—they are how people remember things. The NDIS had the great good fortune to be well named in the first instance, with a non-tongue-tripping acronym (more properly, it's an 'initialism'; an acronym is a pronounceable word, like 'ANZUS' or 'radar').

The NDIS did not make it onto the list of ideas reported back by the groups discussing Themes 2, 3, 4 and 6, but the Theme 5 group, discussing Social Inclusion, did number it among their forty-three ideas.

It was their first listed idea, and also the briefest and clearest: 'Develop a National Disability Insurance Scheme'.

Some other ideas were more consistently voted up. Costello had mentioned in his introductory address rent-to-buy schemes to make housing more affordable, which gathered some support, as did various other related ideas, including increasing grants to first-home buyers. Also consistently popular was an idea put forward by Rudd, for one-stop shops to access community services.

One funding idea is of particular interest: placing a 0.25 per cent levy on the incomes of all Australians. It was not suggested in relation to the NDIS—it was suggested as a 'fidelity levy', to ensure decent living conditions for financially disadvantaged aged Australians.

Saturday dawned, and the delegates reconvened. They discussed what they did and did not like about the proceedings. Some felt their ideas were being ignored. Some felt the discussions were too specific; some felt they were too general. The delegates were divided now into seven groups to discuss the ideas further, clarify and refine their thinking, and report back again.

They came back with, collectively, thirty-eight ideas, with some repetition. Repeated most often was support for same-sex marriage, which had not been prominent the day before. A year later, in April 2009, when the Rudd government kept its promise and responded individually to all 962 ideas enumerated in the so-called Government Response, this idea was unequivocally disavowed, on the grounds of the public's 'widely held view that marriage is between a man and a woman'. Well, they got that wrong.

Another refrain was the lack of established human rights. The support for a human rights charter was strong throughout the groups—as it happened, Shorten was pushing a United Nations convention for the rights of people with disability through parliament at that very moment.

There was one significant idea missing from the thirty-eight submitted: the National Disability Insurance Scheme. It had not rated a single mention.

The now-seven groups in the Community stream came back together to form one group for the Final Plenary session, further refining their ideas. The thirty-eight ideas became twenty-six. No NDIS among them. So, what happened?

The so-called Final Report of the summit, issued a month later, notes: 'In her concluding remarks, co-chair Minister Plibersek asked the group for agreement to include the National Disability Insurance Scheme as an idea for further work and consideration. There were no objections to this proposal.'

The idea could have dropped off the summit agenda there and then. Plibersek's plea was a modest one—not to accept or endorse the idea, but to acknowledge it needed more work. She asked if anyone objected— objecting is a lot different from endorsing. No one wanted to object. And with that little manoeuvre, the NDIS was back on the agenda.

It was smart politics by Plibersek, who was thinking on her feet. Bill Shorten wasted no time once again adding *Establish an NDIS* to the famed butcher's paper on which the ideas were written.

'I could see this was a big and bold reform, but the whole idea of the summit was to think big and think long term,' Plibersek says. She had been aware of the proposal when the summit started. 'People had pointed out again and again how irrationally disability support was provided. Medicare was demand driven, but disability support was rationed. If there were 1000 wheelchairs to be distributed and you were number 1001, you missed out. There was plenty of awareness of the problem.' The idea was also in the ether, she says, as accident insurance in her home state, New South Wales, was in the process of changing to no-fault lifetime care and support.

Plibersek could see the merit of the NDIS idea and didn't want it to die.

'I didn't want to miss out on further examination of the idea by leaving it off the list. And I didn't want it off the agenda because it was too big an idea. There were so many questions to answer about it. I didn't think it was right to rule it out before having the conversation.'

Many ideas had bitten the dust—partly because a new government will also have many ideas of its own—leaving many delegates deflated and disappointed. 'We were in government for the first time in many years, there were lots of ideas floating about, and so many more at the summit,' says Plibersek. 'Quite often it's hard to believe these big things are possible until they actually happen.'

Many delegates accused the chairs of running their own agendas. Costello was one such accused. 'I didn't hear the words "gambling" or "poker machine" at any stage of my time there,' delegate Father Chris Riley, from the community organisation Youth Off the Streets, told *The Australian*. 'I don't know how that got in.'

Plibersek was asked to comment—not on her getting the NDIS back on the agenda, but on Costello's pet topic, gambling. Her office said the facilitators had done all they could to make sure delegates were heard. No one, not a single person, had complained about the late addition of the NDIS, which, of course, didn't actually make it into the final twenty-six ideas, but was still alive as an idea to be considered.

The most important thing, however, had been achieved—the National Disability Insurance Scheme was on the nation's agenda.

∽

The government issued its Initial Report from the 2020 summit, a forty-page document, as the summiteers were headed to the airport. It gave a good but necessarily brief run-down of events and ideas. And there it was—'Another specific idea was the concept of a National Disability Insurance Scheme for people who experience catastrophic injury during their life.'

The proposal had explicitly referred to those born with an injury, not just those who were injured. There is a big difference—the changed wording excludes all those born with a disability.

When supporters of the disability insurance scheme idea opened the so-called Final Report, issued a month later, they did so with trepidation. Had the idea survived? Had the wording been corrected? Rudd had made no mention of the NDIS in his statement accompanying this report, and it was not figuring in newspaper stories.

The Final Report—which was not final, because the even-larger Government Response was to come eleven months later—is comprehensive, a 400-page blockbuster documenting the ideas proposed at the summit.

It noted that an NDIS was one of four big ideas put forward by the Community stream. Other than that, not much.

Again, the focus was limited. The wording had not been corrected, as had been requested by the proposal's submitter. And that's it.

It might not seem an auspicious start, but sometimes the important thing in politics is to get a topic on the agenda, and to get something into print. That alone can serve as a starting point. That much had been achieved by the person who pre-submitted the idea.

Rudd had promised a response to each and every one of the 962 ideas identified as coming out of the summit. He duly responded, one year later. The prime minister set the tone early: 'None of us who gathered at Parliament House for the summit could have foreseen the severity of the global economic downturn that was even then beginning to develop.'

He was referring, of course, to the global financial crisis (GFC), yet another economic headwind emanating from Wall Street's wind tunnel, brought about essentially by low-income American borrowers with low financial literacy defaulting on their home loans, given to them during the high-spirited atmosphere of an enduring rise in the housing market. These loans had, in essence, been spliced into smaller pieces and packaged with other loans, and then sold on the financial markets as AAA cannot-fail securities to organisations all over the world that invested shareholder funds—municipal governments, nurses' pension funds and the like. The disaster affected virtually every country in the world and every bank, spreading panic in the market as banks and other institutions tried to sell these securities. This sent share markets plummeting, condemning some major economies to the worst and longest recession since the Great Depression. More misery inflicted on the world by America not regulating its banks.

Australia escaped the worst of it, thanks largely to treasurer Wayne Swan following the advice of treasury and its head, Ken Henry, to 'go hard and go homes'—putting $900 into the pockets of Australians and urging them to spend the nation out of recession. Swan also moved swiftly to guarantee bank deposits, which forestalled the panic that had gripped the United Kingdom and other places. The combination of measures worked.

If you were to read newspaper reports from 23 April 2009, the day following the Rudd government's response to the 962 ideas, you would search in vain for the NDIS. For it was not one of the nine—*nine!*—ideas that the government had adopted. Which fell short of the dozen Rudd had nominated in his opening address. Or the 10 000 or so submitted.

In the government's response, the NDIS was listed under the ideas to which it would give further thought: 'The Government will consider the development of an insurance model to meet the costs of long-term care for people with disabilities in conjunction with the development of the National Disability Strategy.'

At least the wording had been corrected, thanks to some judicious lobbying. But that was it.

✃

The question remains: just how did the NDIS get on the agenda of the 2020 summit in the first place?

It was there thanks to a submission filed to the summit before proceedings started. The submission, 'Disability reform: from crisis welfare to a planned insurance model', was co-authored by Bruce Bonyhady and Helen Sykes, and was born from the most terrible circumstances.

Helen Sykes had a friend by the name of Robyn, who had a son named James Macready-Bryan. On his twentieth birthday, Friday 13 October 2006, after attending the awards night for Carey Old Boys under 19s at Hawthorn's Geebung Polo Club in Melbourne, James headed into the city, meeting a mate at Flinders Street Station. Before too long, they were assaulted on the street by several offenders. James had his head bashed into bluestone paving, then fled down a dead-end alley and was attacked again. When he fell to the ground, his head slapped the concrete. He was left with lifelong brain injuries, in a permanently and totally incapacitated state. He never got to start the arts/law degree he had been accepted into. Had he incurred his injuries at work or in a car accident, he would have been covered. As it was, all the care and all the expense fell to his parents—which is why Helen Sykes started the James Macready-Bryan Foundation. But she wanted to do more.

Bruce Bonyhady was an economist, formerly a treasury official heading the International Economic Conditions Section, before becoming chief economist at National Mutual. He changed course, and was at this time chair of Philanthropy Australia and also of Yooralla, the largest and best-known disability support agency in Victoria. The change in his life's direction came in 1987, after the birth of his first son, who had cerebral palsy. Two more sons were to follow, the third of whom also had the condition.

Bonyhady, too, wanted to do more. The turning point came for him one day around 2005, when he was at an early intervention centre that Yooralla ran in Endeavour Hills, in Melbourne's outer east. He was sitting with the mother of a boy with disability, and she wanted to know why her son couldn't get the early intervention services he needed. 'She was newly arrived in Australia,' Bonyhady recalls. 'And I went into this long explanation about our funding, how we were trying to sort of stretch the money as far as we could, we knew it was inadequate. And when I walked to my car, I was just appalled by the way I had answered her question, because here was me, with all my connections and privilege and education, and I just justified what we were doing, justified the status quo. I was appalled at my inability to address her needs. And that, that was the watershed moment where I started to think about what we should be doing, as opposed to what we were doing. I thought it was shocking. I was determined to try and find a solution. I had no clear idea what it might be. So that was how it started.'

What linked Bonyhady to Sykes was a friend of his who sat on the James Macready-Bryan Foundation board. Bonyhady also sat on the board of the Disability Housing Trust, which was chaired by Brian Howe.

Brian Howe was a former Labor politician. Elected in 1977 to the Melbourne seat of Batman (named for the syphilitic publican we met earlier and since renamed Cooper, after Indigenous leader William Cooper), he served until 1996, holding various ministries relating to social policy. Born in Melbourne in 1936 and educated at Melbourne High, he was a man with a social conscience, who, like Tim Costello, travelled overseas to study theology—in his case, the United States, rather than Switzerland, and he was a Methodist, rather than a Baptist. While there, he became involved in the civil rights and anti-poverty movements. Post politics, he has lectured at the University of Melbourne and Princeton, maintaining his interest in social reform.

Bonyhady initiated a conversation with Howe about improving the disability sector at large. Bonyhady recalls: 'So I went and saw Brian and he said to me, "Look, stop thinking about this as welfare, think about it in terms of investment and insurance." My background professionally is as an economist, and I'd worked in treasury, and then gone out into the private sector and worked in funds management and insurance—so when he said, "Look at this as an insurance scheme," I knew exactly what he meant. Which was that if we all paid a small amount, then those who needed this scheme would get the support they needed. You know, it's a low risk; the risk of severe and permanent disability early in life is low. Obviously, as we age the risk increases until the time that we all experience disability if we live long enough. Talking with Brian was the lightbulb moment. From that point I began to explore that idea, how insurance could be applied to disability. So I asked Brian who I should I talk to, and I followed them all up. Eventually I got to John Walsh, who was fundamentally involved in the New South Wales no-fault accident compensation scheme. He'd authored, with some others, the so-called Blue Book, which was a proposal to commonwealth and state treasuries to expand the remit of state accident compensation schemes and workplace schemes and medical insurance to a national no-fault scheme. So, I said to John, "Look, can we do this for all disabilities?" And his response was if we can get the data, we can calculate the cost, using the same actuarial approach as he was using to calculate the costs of no-fault accident compensation schemes. But John's Blue Book idea didn't get traction nationally until Labor was elected in 2007 and Bill [Shorten] was appointed the parliamentary secretary for disability services, and who then started to reach out to everybody.'

With a background in the treasury, which had brought him insight into how policy is developed and what is needed to transform an idea into policy, plus work experience with long-term funds, and lived experience of disability, Bonyhady was uniquely placed to develop the big picture. 'Having started my career in the public service, in treasury, and worked there for eight or nine years, I had an understanding of how Canberra operated, and also had an understanding of how treasury thinks, so I knew of the need to frame this not just as a welfare reform, but also as an economic reform. Which it was.'

What the economist in Bonyhady saw was a 'classic case of market failure'—there was no insurance available. And yet, it was a classic case of insurance applying—one in which the whole population is at risk. 'The consequences of major disability on those directly affected and their families are enormous. And so, if we all pay a small amount, then we can insure us all—and it is the most efficient and effective way, as a society, to support people with disabilities,' he told *The Conversation*.

So Bonyhady went off and researched. And thought. And made contacts. 'Brian remained very influential throughout. He had vast experience as a government minister, and he was someone I could always go and talk to. At various key points, I would go and talk to him about this problem or that problem, and how to solve them.'

Brian Howe rang his old comrade Jenny Macklin, who had done research work for him in the 1970s and 1980s, and requested a meeting. 'I met Jenny in the Parliamentary Library in the late 1970s,' Howe recalls. 'At the time, the Victorian government was signing up with Alcoa for their smelter. I got Jenny to look at the aluminium industry and electricity prices, and she wrote a terrific paper. So I thought Jenny was terrific.'

Their working relationship was a long one. In 1981 Macklin had moved on to work at the Labor Resource Centre, of which Howe was the chair. She became a ministerial consultant in the Hawke and Keating years, and was director of the National Health Strategy and then the Urban and Regional Development Review—both times reporting to Howe as her minister.

Macklin happily acknowledges him as her mentor—culminating in her being elected to parliament in 1996, the year he left it. Howe spent five years as deputy prime minister under Hawke and Keating; Macklin was deputy leader in opposition from 2001 to 2006, and was on the same trajectory to be deputy prime minister—until the Rudd–Gillard challenge ousted the Beazley–Macklin team. She had urged caucus to vote for her and Beazley at that time, arguing that Gillard was not a suitable deputy, as she had leadership ambitions of her own.

Macklin recalls: 'Brian Howe, as I mentioned, whom I'd known since 1979, requested a meeting with me and I had huge respect for Brian's policy nous, so of course I quickly agreed. It started with a meeting in February 2008 not long after the 2007 election. Brian brought Bruce Bonyhady with him.

'It all started with trust. I trusted Brian Howe and that trusting relationship enabled a good idea to germinate. At the meeting, Brian said we're thinking about this the wrong way. He wanted us to change our thinking on disability reform, to approach it as an insurance issue rather than a welfare matter,' Macklin recalled in 2019, delivering a speech at her residental college at the University of Melbourne, International House, after having quit parliament.

'Brian said that disability should be seen as a risk issue because anyone could be born with a disability or at any time any one of us can acquire a disability, and the most logical response to that risk was to create a long-term social insurance scheme that covered disability.

'Two central ideas emerged from that meeting. First, that disability is for a lifetime. Therefore, the community should take a lifelong approach to providing care and support. Second, taking an insurance approach to lifelong care and support would allow the community to share the cost of the risk of disability.'

Says Bonyhady: 'The other thing Brian did that was incredibly important was to personally introduce me to Jenny Macklin, in February 2008. Jenny was the senior minister, and remained minister right through the Rudd–Gillard–Rudd government, and became the minister for disability reform. Brian knew Jenny very well, as she had worked for him. And in most big reforms such as this, luck plays a part. You know, she deeply trusted Brian, and Brian and I have a very close relationship. I was introduced to her as someone who could be trusted by Brian. And so, you know, hundreds of people come to see ministers and they've all got a pet idea. Going to see Jenny with Brian and having his endorsement gave it immediate credibility. That created an environment in which I had access. Access is critical to reform.'

The day of their February meeting was, indeed, a big day. It was 13 February, Apology Day, the first sitting day of the forty-second parliament of Australia. After every day of her first eleven years as a member of parliament having been spent in opposition, Macklin's first day in power in parliament was momentous beyond reckoning.

'It was such a significant day,' says Macklin. 'A massive day. I'd done so much work on the Apology. The Apology was at nine o'clock in the morning. It was the first day of the parliament, so there was question time. The meeting with Bruce and Brian was in the afternoon, so it must have been after question time.'

'Yes,' says Bonyhady, 'Jenny had been completely involved in the Apology that morning, and all the preparations for it. So you can just imagine these two people who go into her office in the afternoon to say, "We want to talk about disability insurance." But she had the bandwidth. What's even more remarkable is that she gave a lecture years later that identified the day as that day, and I thought, *Oh*. I was so mono-focused, I could not have told you ten years later that that was the day of the Apology. To be able to switch from all the emotion of that day to a different topic, a technical issue, a complete re-framing of disability funding and services and everything, really ... I'm still gobsmacked.'

～

Bill Shorten made his maiden speech to parliament the next day.

His work on what would become the NDIS had started even earlier, in January, when he cold-called Bonyhady.

'Bill called me in January 2008,' Bonyhady remembers. 'I can tell you where I was—I was in the north of Tasmania at the mouth of the Tamar River, at an aquarium. The mobile phone rings. It's Bill Shorten. Oh, okay. He said, "I want to talk to you." I said, "Sorry, I'm in Tasmania." "When are you back?" "Monday." "Can I see you Monday?"'

In his maiden speech, Shorten said, 'innovation, knowledge and creativity—those are the drivers of economic growth around our world. Those are the drivers that can unlock the full potential of our fellow Australians. Now, more than ever, we need Australians to be educated, skilled and motivated. And we need them to be healthy and engaged.'

That applied perhaps especially to those with disability. 'I am honoured that my prime minister has appointed me as a parliamentary secretary with special responsibility for people with a disability. I am excited by the opportunity to help empower another section of the community, not so people with disability receive special treatment, but so they receive the same treatment as everybody else—the rights which are theirs, with the dignity that they deserve. I believe the challenge for government is not to fit people with disabilities around programs but for programs to fit the lives, needs and ambitions of people with disabilities. The challenge for all of us is to abolish once and for all the second-class status that too often accompanies Australians living with disabilities.

'In this great country, if I were another skin colour or if I were a woman and could not enter a shop, ride a bus, catch an aeroplane or get a job, there would be a hue and cry—and deservedly so—but if I am in a wheelchair or have a mental illness or an intellectual disability then somehow the same treatment is accepted.

'Why should I be told to be grateful to receive charity rather than equality? ... It should go without saying that all of us demand equal treatment for those living with disabilities ... I believe our institutions will have to rethink the way they do things ... This week has shown us all the real meaning of the politics of hope.'

The disability sector is very active, attending closely to developments in its field. Listening to the MP who was now serving it, the sector would have had cause to believe it had a champion.

'How do we get this on the agenda?'

That was the question occupying Bill Shorten's mind—the same question that Jenny Macklin and Bruce Bonyhady had considered after their initial meeting.

Then the perfect vehicle sailed over the horizon and into view: the 2020 summit.

Bonyhady had been talking with Shorten and someone else the minister had tapped for his knowledge in the area—actuary John Walsh. Everyone was thinking the same thing: the Australia 2020 Summit.

They all knew the prime minister had a penchant for big ideas.

'There's nothing so subversive as an idea,' says Shorten. 'You can put up a door to stop physical intrusion, you can build a prison with bars, have a moat full of crocodiles, but an idea can get in through the cracks. Powerful ideas are seductive. I'd already formed that idea that we needed an NDIS. I knew I needed mandating hooks. So I wanted a mandate from the summit.'

Bonyhady applied—along with 8000 other Australians—to be a delegate to the summit, but missed out. There was not one leader from the disability sector in attendance. That did not deter him.

'None of us were invited to the 2020 summit,' Bonyhady recalls, 'so we got the list of delegates, and we wrote to everyone and contacted everyone on that list that we knew. If no one was going to take our idea to the summit as their top idea, we knew we were going to be, at best, their second idea. So we figured that going into the summit, we'd be somewhere worse than position 1001, but somehow it emerged ... It was undoubtedly the big idea of the 2020 summit.'

And that was how delegates to the summit got to read in some detail about this big new idea, the National Disability Insurance Scheme. Bonyhady recalls writing the submission and thinking, *This thing has to have a name.* 'I coined the term "NDIS" for the summit. I thought about what it was: it was national, it was for disability, it was an insurance scheme.'

The idea also got a little media attention before the summit. Journalist Jo Chandler at the *Age* had written movingly about James Macready-Bryan. Shortly before the summit, she spoke again to Helen Sykes, who outlined the proposal to her.

The paper by Bonyhady and Sykes argued the case for an insurance model, along the lines of the one suggested by Howe. It contended that the cost of caring for people with disabilities was, in essence, a very large unfunded liability, which would only continue to increase. In this respect, the economic argument for the scheme was similar to the problem identified by the Hawke–Keating government in the 1980s: when you crunched the demographic numbers, it was clear that eventually the age pension would not be viable—it would weigh down the budget as demographics changed, bringing about an imbalance between those working (whose number was declining as a proportion of the population) and those not working (the proportion of which was increasing). Simply put, there would not be enough workers to support those who were not working. That led to the creation of compulsory superannuation as we know it.

'The time is right to reform the disability sector,' the NDIS summit proposal read, 'to shift from the current crisis-driven welfare approach to a planned and fully funded National Disability Insurance Scheme that will underwrite sustained, significant, long-term improvements in meeting the needs of people with disabilities and their families.

'The projected increase in the proportion of the population with disabilities and declining informal support through unpaid carers will lead to very large increases in the costs of disability, which under present arrangements will add to government outlays.

'We need to plan ahead before the current unmet need and under-met need becomes overwhelming ... To cover the growing costs of disability, which is a risk faced by everyone in the community, there needs to be a fully funded universal National Disability Insurance Scheme. It could be funded from a number of sources, including as a special supplement to the Medicare levy.'

The paper argued that a no-fault insurance model would vastly increase early intervention, which greatly improves outcomes, and lowers costs in the long term. It maintained that such a model would let those with disability live a life as much like everyone else's as possible, which, of course, brings its own economic rewards for them and for the wider community. Such a scheme 'would be equitable and enable people with disabilities and their families to be in control, make choices and plan their lives with confidence'.

The submission said that an insurance model for disability, be it acquired or innate, would give families confidence that the lifelong needs of their disabled family member would be met, which would vastly increase quality of life for all. Many parents lived in dread of their own death because of the consequences it would have for their children. That dread—'midnight anxiety', Shorten calls it—would be alleviated.

It also argued that the scheme would remove the crises in the system, stabilise funding and underwrite lifelong improvements in meeting the needs of those with disability.

A model of clarity, and superbly succinct, the proposal outlined the scheme clearly. The extraordinary thing is that the thinking in it remained constant for years on end thereafter; the NDIS we got, even down to the funding model, is the one described there, which all the people at the summit got to read.

The proposal was good enough to convince delegates on the first day, even if they *seemed* to have forgotten it the next. No matter—the idea was now in circulation. It was on the agenda.

No matter how strong an idea is, it can't defend itself. An idea needs its champion. When Bonyhady scanned the names of summit delegates, he found someone he knew: Gina Nancy McGregor Anderson.

'I was CEO of Philanthropy Australia, and my chairman was Bruce Bonyhady,' Anderson recalls. 'I worked very closely with Bruce on philanthropy and other things. I got selected to go, and we all had to take an idea. There were no disability advocates to the summit, and so I said to Bruce, "Would you like me to take the NDIS?" and he said, "Would you?", and I said, "Of course I would."'

Delegates were selected as knowledgeable individuals, not as organisational representatives, but, again, no high-profile disability advocates were present and no one can recall there being delegates with a disability (although many disabilities are invisible). It is a telling fact about where disability was in the national consciousness.

'But before I took it there, I checked the idea with people,' Anderson says. 'I was up in the country at the time and I went around to various friends, none of whom had a child with disability, and I asked them,

"What about this for a project?" And universally they said to me, "That's a great idea. That's really important, Gina." So I went back to Bruce and I said, "Yep, I'll take the project on."

'There was a whole lot of scurrying going on behind the scenes. Bill Shorten was worded up on it. One of the key things about this whole process was that Bruce Bonyhady clearly understood that the best way to get this project up was to give away his power of ownership. He empowered Bill to take it. Bruce said to me, "I don't care who claims it, Gina, I want the thing up." That was a big learning curve for me—if you really want to get something up, pull your ego right out of it and you empower everyone else.

'We were all in streams; I was in the Community stream. When the prime minister came around, Kevin Rudd, to see how all of the streams were progressing, Bill facilitated me to put forward my idea. It was fairly well orchestrated. So it got an airing in the presence of Rudd. A couple of others were put up. Ahmed Fahour was first. He put up an idea about a social impact fund, if I recall correctly, and then it was my turn. I presented, it was brief, a couple of minutes; Kevin said thank you, and Bill wrote it down on the, what was it—butcher's paper.'

Gina Anderson's group within the Community stream wasn't the only one to recommend the idea. Her memory is that on the second morning, the idea was reconfirmed.

'What I remember was our group emphasising to Tanya [Plibersek] that this program was preventative. Don't be funding at the bottom of the cliff, start the funding at the top. You know, early intervention. These are experienced activists we're talking about. It's about putting the money there up front, so that people can have the ability to work, to have a functioning life. Our group was looking for preventative measures. This was one.'

But the idea did drop off the agenda on the second day—only to be saved at the last minute by Plibersek, aided and abetted by Shorten, who quickly scribbled it onto the butcher's paper a second time.

The thousand delegates reassembled in parliament's Great Hall. Plibersek then presented the findings from her group—including this grand idea of how to fund and reform services for people with disability. She recalls getting a warm welcome.

Gina Anderson remembers too. 'The big thing I remember most was when the NDIS was read out, there was spontaneous applause from the audience. And a friend of mine, who had been in the Agriculture stream, who was sitting next to me, leaned over and said, "That's a fantastic idea." He didn't realise I had brought it. And so I rang Bruce and said to him that was the big thing—the spontaneous applause from the room said, *This is a really good idea*. And I think that sort of endorsement from people who were not part of the disability fraternity, just the general public, I think was very powerful for Kevin and Bill. They heard that, particularly Bill, and they knew that this had legs. That was right at the end, in the Great Hall, with everyone present, and Hugh Jackman led us through [the Paul Kelly song] "From Little Things Big Things Grow".

'People just clapped. That was the overriding sentiment I took away from the summit.'

On the Tuesday morning straight after the summit, Melbourne ABC listeners heard Shorten on the radio. He was talking up the NDIS. He had chosen his journalist well—morning host Jon Faine was previously a lawyer. He could, with no difficulty, conduct an intelligent conversation on the inadequacies and inequities of compensation law as against the superiority of compensation schemes, making it all comprehensible to people as they sat in traffic on the freeways or plugged in their head-phones on trains or trams.

'The thing that has hit me very clearly [since being handed disability services], and a lot of people already know this, is that it's always a crisis in disability,' Shorten told Faine. 'Now, a lot of really good people over a number of years have raised at the state level, but never nationally, a lifetime care scheme for the catastrophically injured ... so what's being looked at is the idea of a national scheme ... What we want to do is find as many resources as possible to support these people. We could do this, give people a safety net if confronted by catastrophe. What was good about the summit is it drew attention to ideas—my office has been working with a range of state representatives because we think this is an idea whose time has come.'

The summit had done its job—it was the platform from which this big idea sprang. 'Maybe a thousand flowers did bloom,' says Shorten, 'but I backed one sentence—"Establish an NDIS"—and it's the one idea that came out of the summit. And then I made that my primary document.'

Days later, Shorten pulled an ace from his sleeve.

He announced the formation of DIG—the Disability Investment Group—which he had discussed with Bonyhady on the Monday after that cold call. Its brief was to look for ways to get private investment into the disability sector—exactly the sort of new thinking he had referenced in his maiden speech. The problem was clear: the funding for disability was inadequate, but asking treasury for more was not going to get the job done.

Shorten, through Macklin, managed to secure $1.5 million in funding for DIG to do its work. It was a heavy-hitting team, with some of the smartest money minds in the country. Bonyhady, who had, of course, been looking for a solution ever since his conversation with a migrant mother about her boy, was part of DIG, which, ultimately, did a lot more than its brief. 'We were given this task of how to invest in disability,' says Bonyhady. 'What DIG did in the end was focus on what became the NDIS.'

That's where they were headed; but first, where had this idea come from?

'THE INEQUALITY OF LUCK'

———

ALL BIG IDEAS have a history, even a prehistory, and such is the case with the idea of a national disability insurance scheme. Intriguingly, there is a straight line through to the NDIS going back through multiple Australian governments, especially Gough Whitlam's, all the way to the newly unified Germany in the nineteenth century. 'It goes all the way back to Bismarck,' says Bruce Bonyhady.

Otto von Bismarck was born into the Prussian landholding class in 1815. Educated in agriculture, fluent in five languages, he became a politician and diplomat, culminating in his masterminding the unification of Germany in 1871. He wrote its constitution and became its first chancellor.

Germany was a country of political ideology, in which the competing classes had well-formed ideas about themselves and their own interests. That was as true of Bismarck as it was of anyone else. He was a Junker, a country squire, and in his political infancy, it was those class interests that he set out to protect. The world of the Junkers was predicated upon the labour of peasants; it was a rural economy, where conditions had remained largely unchanged for centuries—and the powers that be were happy for them to stay that way. The enemy, it was clear to Bismarck, were the socialists (and anarchists), whose class interests were in conflict with his. Rats, he called them.

In the 1880s, the second decade of his rule of Germany, Bismarck feared the rising popularity of the various Marxists, socialists and anarchists, all of whom deplored capitalism to greater or lesser degrees. By this time a mature, experienced statesman, he had as much enmity for the socialists as ever, but was an intelligent, pragmatic leader who knew when to bend, lest the state break. His response was to concede what he could to wean the workers from these other ideologies.

The result was a series of legislative acts across the decade that gave workers comprehensive insurance against illness, unemployment and work injuries. Pensions, too, were established, as virtually his last act before being forced out of power. Disability—in the sense of becoming disabled and unable to work—was covered. Germany thus became the first welfare state, thanks to a leader forestalling the advance of socialism. The system put in place became the model for all other nations.

Indeed, it was this legislation that UK prime minister David Lloyd George looked to in 1911 when enacting the National Insurance Act. This was an insurance scheme against illness that was the beginning of Great Britain's version of the welfare state.

Political developments in Britain were watched closely in faraway Australia. That same year, Joseph Cook, who had been head of the Anti-Socialist Party and two years later would become prime minister, told parliament: 'The more I think of it the more convinced I am that we must come ultimately to a form of national insurance'.

The idea was revisited during the 1922 election campaign, championed by Country Party leader Earle Page, the fast-talking surgeon-cum-dairy farmer, who formed a coalition government with the Nationalist Party, led by Stanley Bruce. A royal commission to flesh out the idea was put in place the following year, and reported, somewhat leisurely, four years later, after an intervening election. The government had been re-elected in the meantime, and enabling legislation was introduced late in its term, in 1928.

The insurance scheme would cover many things—child allowance, widows' allowance, orphans' allowance, superannuation, widows' superannuation—but the subjects that concern us here are the sickness allowance and disablement allowance. Sickness allowance was payable to anyone in the scheme who could not work because of 'some specific disease or some physical or mental incapacity'. The wording was broad. Tellingly, it extended beyond injury to disease, be it of the mind or body. Sickness allowance transformed into disability allowance if the person's incapacity extended beyond twenty-six weeks. To be sure, the bill did not cover those who were disabled from birth and who had never worked and thus never paid insurance, but it did cover all manner of disability. The legislation, however, failed to pass.

It had been predicated upon providing unemployment benefits, which were conspicuously absent from the bill, set aside for consideration elsewhere. *The Age* took a dismal view of proceedings in its reporting of the matter on 18 September 1928, following the introduction of the bill the week prior, just two months in advance of the next election.

'Though the national insurance scheme has been introduced as a bill,' the *Age* report began, 'it may be assumed that its sponsors do not expect it to become law in its present form. Before any further progress can be made a general election will be held; thereafter the measure will have to be re-introduced for the consideration of a new Parliament. The present ministry in thus adroitly evading a present responsibility confirms the suspicion long entertained that in the matter of national insurance its interest has been tepid. It is more than five years since the question came prominently before the country and the Bruce–Page ministry with some show of enthusiasm appointed a royal commission to prepare a scheme. The commission's inquiry was thorough and its proceedings unhurried. Before it had finished its labours the [1925] election took place, and the promise of social insurance, enabling the worker to be insured against unemployment, figured conspicuously in the Prime Minister's policy speech. About a year later the commission produced a report and recommendations. It has taken the government the better part of two years to draft a measure and submit it to Parliament. During that period there was no stress of legislative business; Parliament was at no times over-worked; there were abundant opportunities for the introduction, full consideration and passage of a bill covering the whole wide question. The subject was deferred, however, until the last minute. To introduce a bill in Parliament's expiring hours with no intention of attempting to make a law may enable the ministry to plead that it has not forgotten its pre-election promises, but it can hardly be claimed that this procedure constitutes redemption of a pledge.'

Newspapers were different back then.

Stanley was re-elected, but his government lasted barely a year, and the insurance scheme never came into being. Labor's Jim Scullin was elected—and days later the Great Depression began. Pity the unemployed.

The idea was revived in 1937, when Joseph Lyons, prime minister and leader of the United Australia Party, campaigning for re-election, promised a national health insurance scheme as in the United Kingdom. He won, and legislative work began all over again. The scheme ran into opposition from the medical fraternity, which succeeded in stalling proceedings by way of another royal commission. The attorney-general was Robert Menzies; the crown solicitor, who did some of the drafting of the bill for the scheme, was Fred Whitlam, whose surname would become more well known, thanks to his son.

Earle Page, the erstwhile supporter of the scheme, was still the leader of the Country Party, which was, once more, the junior coalition member. He declared they could not support the scheme as it was too expensive (a theme echoed in later years, as we shall see), the excuse being that more money needed to flow to defence as the clouds of war were gathering on the horizon. Infuriated, Menzies, who had supported the scheme, resigned in dismay, saying that such a delay would set back the cause for another generation. All of this made an impression on the younger Whitlam, Gough, a law student at the time. In fact, it became a lifelong obsession for him.

There were also very serious consequences in the near term, as Lyons suffered a heart attack and died before a deputy had been appointed to replace Menzies. The ensuing tumult played a role in destabilisng the government, which actually fell during wartime, after Menzies had taken Lyons' role as PM. In the midst of World War II, Labor's John Curtin promised unemployment benefits in the campaign of 1943 and they were enacted the following year, with payments beginning the year after that. All very well—but those with disability would still have to wait.

Whitlam by this time was no longer a law student. Having served in the war, he worked as a lawyer, then was elected in 1952 to the House of Representatives in the seat of Werriwa (the Indigenous name for Canberra's Lake George, which was within the seat's original boundaries). Whitlam was more aware than most of the inequities of compensation law, having done his share of negligence cases in the courts.

The first time he espoused the idea of national insurance compensation, as he records in *The Whitlam Government 1972–1975*, was at a caucus meeting in the run-up to the 1954 election. Labor leader 'Doc' Evatt had opened the floor to discussion, inviting members to give their ideas to carry to the electorate. Whitlam spoke up, suggesting a national compensation scheme. He argued that it could build on the success of the 1946 referendum, which had given the commonwealth the power to provide the widows' pension, child allowances, unemployment benefits and other such social goods, which Curtin had enacted. Evatt took note—but when he left the meeting, his notes remained on the table. It turned out that the campaign strategy and policy had already been decided. An odd response, given Evatt's dedication to human rights— he was the president of the United Nations General Assembly when it voted in the Universal Declaration of Human Rights.

Whitlam took up the theme again in his Chifley Lecture, delivered at the University of Melbourne in 1957, in which he outlined the various inadequacies and inequities of negligence law, and how those who suffered injury could so easily be denied compensation.

He took up the case again in 1959. Speaking in estimates hearings on 29 September 1959, he addressed what he termed 'the most prevalent and the least appropriate form of litigation in Australia'—cases seeking damages after car accidents.

Whitlam said that half of the cases brought in the various state supreme, district and county courts were seeking compensation for injuries arising from car accidents. Leaning on the work of the commonwealth statistician, he recorded the fact that in 1958–59, there were 39 473 accidents involving casualties, resulting in 2146 people killed and 52 213 injured. (That's a death toll almost twice that of 2022, when there were seven times as many vehicles on the roads.) He said that compulsory third-party insurance amounted to £16 064 000 and that total payouts came to £14 202 000.

With typical clarity, he advanced his argument. 'I pass now to the appropriateness of such litigation. It is uncertain whether a plaintiff will recover damages. He has to establish the negligence of the defendant, and very often he has to show that he himself did not contribute to the accident by his own negligence. A plaintiff may have to sue two or more defendants and succeed against only one or some of them. It is also uncertain how much damages he will recover. He may recover only a lump sum, which may be quite inappropriate, for instance, if a woman plaintiff shortly afterwards remarries or if there is inflation in subsequent years. Again, practically always, expense is attached to the present procedure.'

Whitlam continued, warming to the task, and his magisterial sonority echoes across the decades. 'Thirdly, there is delay in these cases. The standard time that elapses before a verdict is secured by a plaintiff in

New South Wales is two years. Throughout that period, not only does the plaintiff have to go without any compensation for his pain and suffering or his loss of income or his out-of-pocket expenses, but hospitals and doctors have to wait for payment for a similar period.

'Again, there are many anomalies in this form of litigation. The owner–driver cannot recover damages for an accident which was caused solely by his own negligence. His wife cannot recover damages, although his parents, his children, his mistress or a complete stranger to whom he had given a lift can recover damages.

'Contributory negligence is a complete defence in New South Wales, however little that negligence contributed to the accident ... Then one still meets, though infrequently, the defence of "inevitable accident". If an accident would have happened, anyhow, on the roads, irrespective of any driver's negligence, nobody gets damages for the injuries arising from it. Then there is the defence of the voluntary assumption of risk where the person who accepts a lift from a driver whom he knows to be under the influence of alcohol cannot secure damages if he is injured as the result of the negligence of that driver.

'To sum up, all motor owners have to pay insurance to cover damages arising from road accidents. There is no certainty, however, that the victim of a road accident will receive damages. The only certainty is that he will have to wait for damages of a conjectural amount at a conjectural cost.'

Having made the case showing that the current state of affairs was wholly unsatisfactory, Whitlam moved easily to its solution. 'The remedy, I suggest, is that the element of fault should be eliminated ... We have already done this with respect to industrial accidents,' he said, noting that there were many more car accidents than industrial accidents.

'The Commonwealth should, through the Department of Social Services, make periodic payments available to the victims of road accidents or their dependants to give them the same income after the accidents, until the age at which they retire or would have retired as they would have received but for the accident.'

The mechanism for doing this would be appropriating the petrol tax. Doing so, he argued, would remove the delay, the expense and the uncertainty of these cases, which were clogging up the courts.

Whitlam received but a desultory response. It was suggested he make his comments to the royal commission underway in Victoria, into a no-fault accident compensation scheme—which was not legislated until a quarter-century later, in the 1980s.

It needs to be pointed out here that the scheme was to cover accidents—it was a remedy for a law that did not provide a proper remedy. It did not cover disability. But Whitlam would expand the idea.

Come 1971, just such a scheme was part of Labor's platform, thanks to him.

It was a promise Whitlam made to the Australian people when he asked them to vote for him in the 1972 election. 'We will establish a National Compensation Scheme to reduce the hardships imposed by one of the great factors for inequality in society—inequality of luck,' he said.

The promise was again part of his pitch in the 1974 campaign: 'We are determined to place the security, the welfare of those who suffer incapacity through accident or sickness, on a sure and certain basis, on the basis of confidence and freedom from financial anxiety for themselves and their families. Australians should not have to live in doubt or anxiety lest injury or sickness reduce them to poverty.'

Note the presence of one key word: sickness.

All of this was top of mind when Whitlam was elected prime minister the first time, on 2 December 1972. One of his very first acts upon taking up that position was to ring his New Zealand counterpart, Norman Kirk. Whitlam made a special request: he asked that Mr Justice Owen Woodhouse be freed of his duties so that he could come to Australia and do what he had done in New Zealand: namely, oversee the introduction of a no-fault insurance scheme. Whitlam's interest was so keen that in 1970 he had sought out Justice Woodhouse while he was docked in New Zealand during a boat cruise, and then made a point of seeing Woodhouse while paying respects to the NZ prime minister on a visit in January 1973.

Justice Woodhouse was duly relieved of his duties and did indeed come to Australia, where he headed a three-man panel to deliver just such a scheme. The other two were CLD Meares, New South Wales Supreme Court justice; and Patrick S Atiyah, an English lawyer and academic, an expert in the field of tort law and, at the time, a professor at the Australian National University.

As was the way with the Whitlam government, no time was lost. Fifteen months later, the panel submitted its three-volume report, which the prime minister later described as 'one of the most convincing and stimulating reports ever presented to the Parliament', a judgement perhaps only Whitlam was qualified to deliver.

The idea met with stern opposition.

In the front line, predictably, were the lawyers. As can be seen from Whitlam's remarks, negligence suits were a good little earner for quite a few of them. A no-fault scheme would wipe out an awful lot of that work overnight. All the legal fraternity had to do was converse with their learned brethren across the Tasman Sea to discover the effects of such legislation on their earning capacity.

Next came the doctors, some of whom were onto a good thing in writing medico-legal reports for such court cases. They did not want to be denied a meal ticket either. Nor was it uncommon for doctors to charge a higher fee than usual if insurance companies were footing the bill.

Insurance companies stood to lose as well. The above figures from the commonwealth statistician show the money to be made—in round terms, for sixteen dollars coming in, only fourteen dollars was going out, leaving two dollars for the insurer, thank you, m'lord.

If the country's lawyers, doctors and insurance companies are arrayed against a piece of legislation, it will be fighting an uphill battle, no matter how great an idea it might be. That is magnified when these interested parties are well aware of the intended scheme and its implications, while those who would benefit might not even know of its existence.

Sadly, the scheme failed to generate the support that might have been expected from those who would benefit, even when they did know about it.

Those in unions, who had at least long enjoyed coverage via workers compensation, were not prepared to lose what they already had. They were, of course, being advised by law firms who also had a stake in the matter.

Welfare groups failed to wholeheartedly back the scheme either. The model, lacking the intellectual sophistication that characterises the sector today, would have given more compensation to a high earner than to a low earner, and did not fit with their egalitarian thinking.

Even lawyers and unionists within Whitlam's caucus failed to support the proposal.

The scheme would inevitably face legal challenges by the strong vested interests that stood to lose from it. As soon as the opportunity arose, an obstructive Senate raised such concerns and used them to stall the legislation.

In February 1974, as Woodhouse and co. diligently worked away, a major change took place. The terms of reference were extended to inquire whether the scheme should be broadened to all who suffered sickness or 'congenital defect', to use its wording. Bronwyn Morkham says the extension was Woodhouse's idea.

The answer was yes, it should—and that is what Whitlam took to the people when campaigning in the 1974 election. The scheme would not be restricted to compensation for car accidents—it would cover every injury suffered by any person anywhere at any time, *including prenatal injuries*. That is, a scheme that would compensate those born disabled.

As well as recommending that the scheme be open to the disabled, it proposed that assistance be provided for whatever rehabilitation was possible, and compensation. Further, according to Professor Harold Luntz, writing in the *Victoria University of Wellington Law Review* ('Looking Back at Accident Compensation: An Australian Perspective, 2003'), the scheme provided for 'a personal attendant and domiciliary care ... and a comprehensive plan for rehabilitation services'. Rehabilitation was a key part of the scheme.

Having been re-elected in May 1974, Whitlam tabled the first volume of the Woodhouse report on 10 July, and on 26 September the second volume was tabled. A week later, on 3 October, the bill was introduced to parliament, and it was passed by the House three weeks later.

The wording used by the special minister of state, Lionel Bowen, when introducing the bill is unambiguous. 'The scheme envisaged ... embraces injury, congenital disability and sickness,' Bowen told the House. Those suffering a disability were to be rehabilitated (to the extent possible) and compensated via this national insurance scheme. The emphasis was very strongly on rehabilitation—it was always stressed as being the objective, wherever possible.

The scheme was to be introduced in three phased stages. The first stage, from mid-1976, would cover injury and disability from that date on. The second stage, to come in at an unspecified date, would cover injury and disability prior to that date. The Woodhouse report recommended the scheme be financed by a levy on petrol (to the tune of ten cents a gallon, the imperial measure for 4 litres, roughly speaking), but Bowen explicitly left open the possibility that some other means might be found, which treasury was investigating (well, supposedly—Whitlam later wrote that treasury disobeyed orders and failed to do this work).

Whitlam also issued a statement announcing an advisory council, headed by CLD Meares. It noted that 'in the past, the handicapped have been neglected and often isolated. Society has paid far too little attention to their needs. Mr Whitlam said that with the Council's help, the Government would ensure that the handicapped would receive all the assistance and protection which could reasonably be provided, so that they could find a worthwhile place in society.'

And now the trouble began.

The bill advanced to the Senate, where Whitlam did not have a majority, on 30 October. After the second reading, it was referred to the Senate Standing Committee on Legal and Constitutional Affairs, which was to report back within a month.

The Woodhouse committee was certain that any and all constitutional hurdles could be overcome, relying on advice from the solicitor-general. But legal advice could also be had that said the opposite, which was what the Senate committee wanted to hear and did hear.

In his record of events, Whitlam outlines the campaign against the legislation. He writes that the committee was bombarded by submissions—and bombarded by interested parties wishing to make a submission if only they had more time. The insurance companies mounted a campaign of disinformation. Even worse, lawyers got in on the act, for fear of the cases—and fees—they would be denied if damages for negligence were to be awarded without the trouble of court cases. It was all exactly as Whitlam had outlined in 1959. The campaign worked—the committee sought and received extensions until April, then June, then July 1975. 'Charlatans' was the word Whitlam used to describe the legal objectors.

Eventually the committee recommended the bill be withdrawn, redrafted and rewritten, which it was.

And when the legislation was redrafted, the reference to 'congenital disability' was gone. People with disability would not be covered.

The bill was to be resubmitted to parliament for discussion on 11 November 1975. That date will be familiar to most Australians. As we know, events overtook the bill. So it was that the third such attempt to gain national disability insurance failed.

That, however, was not the end of the matter—there was a fourth attempt. Whitlam introduced the redrafted bill to parliament on 24 February 1977, in his capacity as a private member. The Fraser government did not allow it to go to a vote. As to Whitlam, we will let him have the last word: 'For 23 years—from 1954 to 1977—I campaigned against the great inefficiencies and inequities of the existing system. [The campaign's failure] was one of the great disappointments of my life.'

The thing about big ideas, though, is that they do not die. They go into hibernation, until their time comes around again.

In the meantime, they will often get glancing attention here and there. In 1979, when the Whitlam years seemed very far away indeed, Justice Michael Kirby assessed Gough Whitlam the law reformer in the *Federal Law Review*, Vol 10, and, in particular, his national compensation scheme. He wrote: 'We may have to wait for better economic times and a different vehicle before it is introduced.'

There was a very brief flirtation with the idea during the Howard government; a passing thought bubble, really. The context was a crisis in insurance, brought about by the collapse of insurance company HIH, and the supposed increased risk after the September 11 attacks. Overnight, many individuals, companies, organisations and groups such as sporting clubs were without insurance, especially for public liability—injuries to members of the public. Many of those bodies simply had to stall their activities, because insurance either could not be had at all or could be had only at a prohibitive price. This left them totally exposed to a claim if they were not covered by an insurance policy and someone was injured.

In January 2002 the then small business minister, Joe Hockey, was so bold as to suggest that New Zealand's national no-fault compensation scheme could be a model for somesuch here. Comments by Hockey pointing to people being more litigious, as seen in the rising number of claims, and the unpredictability of compensation awarded by the courts, and the cost to small business, indicate his interest was driven more by protecting business than the injured parties, especially as he emphasised capped payouts. The howls of outrage from lawyers could be heard far and wide. The idea went nowhere—but it didn't go away, either.

It resurfaced at the state level before it did at the federal level.

John Della Bosca took up a seat in the New South Wales parliament in 1999, and the Motor Accidents Authority came within his purview. It didn't take long before a case highlighting its deficiencies came before him.

'An older gentleman had some kind of blackout fit while driving down a hill. The car was out of control because he was unconscious and drove into a childcare centre. He was charged and put on trial, and his barrister put in a plea that it was, in legal terms, an inevitable accident [which, as per Whitlam's above comments, would mean no compensation]. And the evidence for that was that he'd never been warned by a doctor, wasn't a diabetic or epileptic, so there was no reason to believe that he could black out. There was no evidence to think he would; it had never happened to him before. So, because he was not at fault, there was coverage for him if he was injured, but no coverage for all these injured kids and teachers, many of whom were severely injured. So, I had to ring his insurer, and I said, "This is a disaster. It's a multimillion-dollar claim, and I know you don't have to pay it, what are you going to do?" And they said, "Don't worry, Minister, we already know, we're paying the claim." So that was fine. I think they knew that if they didn't pay it, it would have been a commercial catastrophe for them as well as a huge problem for the government, because we would have had to step in and pay it out of the Nominal Defendant anyway, but that would have been a huge hassle with treasury and everyone else as well. Anyway, that was just a little kind of issue as to how the insurance system ... wasn't working.'

It needed fixing, and it was fixed. Actuary John Walsh was the man who fixed it. The mechanism was the Motor Accidents (Lifetime Care and Support) Act 2006, which provides for lifelong treatment, rehabilitation and care of those injured in vehicle accidents in New South Wales. It is funded by a levy on car registration (the so-called 'green slip').

'I'd become close to John Walsh because he was the scheme actuary for both the Workers Compensation Commission and the Motor Accidents Authority when I was minister,' Della Bosca recalls.

'John is a pretty big thinker on this stuff. And so, he was certainly already using the terminology "National Disability Insurance Scheme" and he was kind of toying with all the ways it would work.'

Walsh was the top man in his field, eventually becoming a partner at PricewaterhouseCoopers (PwC), one of the world's big four accounting firms, providing all manner of professional services to business and government. He was also Australia's Actuary of the Year in 2001. As Della Bosca notes, he was a big thinker—now that New South Wales, Victoria and Tasmania had no-fault accident schemes, Walsh wanted to expand such a scheme nationally. He was also a long-term thinker—actuaries have to think a long way forward, but Walsh thought backwards as well, through history.

'Whitlam's example was really how I started thinking about all this,' he says, referencing the failed bid to enact a scheme like New Zealand's.

'However, many states did integrate aspects of this in their schemes in the late 1980s: for example, the MAIB [Motor Accidents Insurance Board in Tasmania] and the TAC [Transport Accident Commission in Victoria] in motor injury, and virtually all the states and territories in workers compensation, and there was a continued interest in developing a no-fault long-term care scheme. Over the next years, I continued this interest.'

Walsh saw no reason why these schemes could not go national. That idea became a topic for the Insurance Issues Working Group of Heads of

Treasuries, which commissioned a report on the feasibility and cost of a national no-fault long-term care scheme for such injuries. All these years later, the country is still waiting for it. In its absence, Walsh points out, people over sixty-five who are catastrophically injured, outside of vehicle accidents, are still not covered.

He was also a wide thinker, thinking about how the scheme could be applied beyond vehicle accidents.

Senator Jan McLucas says Della Bosca and Walsh suggested to her prior to the 2007 election that a no-fault scheme be extended to disability—in effect, the same thing as the NDIS—and be a campaign promise. This was too tall an order in the absence of costings and the necessary policy work. Walsh, however, does not recall the meeting.

But, accompanied by Bruce Bonyhady, he did have a meeting about the idea with senior public servants before the 2007 election. 'John and I went to Canberra and met with Jeff Harmer, the head of department of social services, or whatever it was then, and Ken Henry from treasury, so we had already started to put our feelers out.'

Bonyhady credits Whitlam as a foundational thinker and the inspiration for his work. He also acknowledges an American economist. 'The twin idea of universal health insurance and universal disability insurance had been around since the early 1960s, thanks to the work of the American economist Kenneth Arrow, who did the initial work that proved societies would be better off, both socially and economically, to have universal insurance rather than relying on private health insurance. "Welfare in the Face of Uncertainty" was the paper.'

As we know, in October 2007 Bronwyn Morkham's Young People in Nursing Homes Alliance ran a conference recommending just such a scheme. Bonyhady was there, but had to leave early to catch a plane. 'We were talking about an injury scheme. Bruce later took it to the 2020 summit and expanded it to disability,' Morkham says.

For ideas to come to fruition, they have to appear at the right time.

The time just before the 2007 election was almost, but not quite, the right time. But the time was coming.

One of the first things Bill Shorten did upon becoming parliamentary secretary for disability services was to contact his New South Wales counterpart, Della Bosca, who called in John Walsh. Walsh says they 'talked particularly at that first meeting about a National Injury Insurance Scheme, which would be a no-fault scheme for catastrophic injuries'. That was the scheme Shorten was referencing when he spoke with Jon Faine the day after the summit. An idea he and others were expanding.

When Jenny Macklin became a minister in 2007, she was quite consciously working in the shadow of Whitlam. Her life in politics had begun in 1979, the year that Whitlam left parliament. Macklin painted a picture of this continuity in her speech to International House in 2019. First, she noted, all policymakers are influenced by the past; the starting point of any research is what has happened so far.

'Everything started to change with the election of the Whitlam government,' she said, referencing his memorable phrase 'the inequality of luck'.

'Going back to Whitlam, in 1973, they initiated an inquiry into compensation and rehabilitation, which recommended a no-fault compensation scheme. They concluded that the most efficient, cost-effective way to tackle the issue was to provide a national compensation scheme rather than focus on fault. Unfortunately that no-fault scheme was never implemented. As a consequence, hundreds of thousands of Australians were effectively shut out of everyday life for the next forty years. Anyone who acquired or was born with a disability was treated as a second-class citizen, largely dependent on their friends and family. If you had a disability, any low-level support you received was arbitrary.'

Macklin's point was that *'to redefine a problem, you really need to understand your history'*. In the case of disability policy, that history informed our thinking and showed what needed to be done, but that knowledge, of course, was never going to be enough.

'There was excellent work on no-fault accident and catastrophic injury insurance happening in New South Wales under the leadership of actuary John Walsh,' Macklin recalls. 'John was hooked on the potential of insurance models to provide the community the funding required to meet the inevitable long-term increase in demand for disability supports.'

Macklin was right. For a good idea to become policy, much more is needed, as we shall see. The pieces, however, were falling into place. The thinking would only get bigger.

'In 2007, with the election of the Rudd government, I was given the opportunity to build on the policies of Whitlam, Hawke and Keating,' she said.

That opportunity manifested on that bright, historic day, 13 February 2008, when the roles were reversed and Brian Howe entered *her* office, accompanied by Bruce Bonyhady.

The time for this idea had come.

THE LAST FRONTIER

_____

NEW DIRECTIONS HAD noted as far back as the early 1980s that people with disability had begun to speak out. Now, in 2008–09, they were about to be handed a megaphone and a platform, so that their voices could be heard nationally.

The ministerial council that Shorten had immediately set up—the National People with Disabilities and Carer Council (NPDCC)—had started the three groups in the sector talking. Now it had a more specific task: the job of developing a National Disability Strategy. It decided that the voices that needed to be heard were the voices of those with disability; that the people best qualified to offer advice on how the system should be run were those on the receiving end.

The way to do this was by public consultation on a national scale. At its conclusion, there was a report to government, *Shut Out: The Experience of People with Disabilities and Their Families in Australia.* The goal was clearly defined—tell us what the problems are.

Within this story lies another: that of the disability sector itself, and what the NPDCC achieved simply by the fact of its existence and the make-up of its twenty-eight members.

To speak of the 'disability sector' makes it sound like one thing, a unified force. In reality, it was diverse, it was multiple—it variously represented people who had nothing in common with each other, whose disabilities had nothing in common. The funds that the federal government had provided over the years, and self-organisation, meant that eventually most disabilities had a representative group. That had an unintended consequence: those groups were competing for the same resources. The disability sector was not just multiple and diverse, but fragmented and divided. Worse, it was at war with itself.

The reasons for that were historical and essentially simple. The sector was composed of three groups: those with disability, their carers, and the service providers. The interests of one group were often at odds with those of other groups. The way they argued their case was often at odds as well: many believed that the only way forward was to advocate for their rights, that a legal foundation had to be laid to ensure success in arguing this case, no matter the forum. Abstract principles such as rights were of secondary importance, however, to a parent caring for their child, who needed help—physical help, financial help—right here, right now. Carers' pleading often referred to their unbearable burden, while those with disabilities fighting for their rights wanted to be thought of as anything but a burden. Rather, they wanted to be seen as human beings just like any other, but their rights had been left in abeyance, or had been denied them.

These divisions were historical, had become entrenched, and had widened over time.

As Bruce Bonyhady put it: 'You need to realise that the disability sector split in the 1980s. If you go back to the 1950s and 1960s it was parents who primarily spoke for people with disabilities and they formed the disability organisations, and the sector was unified really around the parents. In the 1980s with the disability rights movement, right throughout that period the disability organisations became split. By 2000, you've got the three arms of the sector, it was sort of war, and it wasn't just war at that level, it was also a battle between the different disabilities groups, and within them. So, people with autism wanted something which people with cerebral palsy didn't want, and wanted something different from people with vision impairment.'

No one had attempted to set in place a divide-and-conquer strategy, but that is what had emerged organically out of the divisions. Those representing people with autism did not want to be associated at that level with those representing mental illness. Those who were arguing for specifics, such as access to assisted technology or greater financial support, were seen by those advocating for rights as missing the bigger picture. And there were differences of strategy: those arguing for rights wanted to win that war, whereas those arguing for assisted technology or financial support wanted to win their war battle by battle.

Sitting as the chair of the council that brought twenty-eight people together, Rhonda Galbally had a bird's-eye perspective.

'The situation was desperate, and families bore the impact,' she says. 'Either they provided care, or none was provided. Many families simply could not keep going. In the 90s, families came together to form the carer movement, and the carers started to campaign strongly and loudly. They saw disability largely from a burden perspective, with family members with disabilities as the burdens. This characterisation was understandable because that was the actual experience of many families, but it alienated the networks of people with disabilities fighting for rights. During the second half of the 1990s and into the twenty-first century, people with disabilities saw the carer movement become well funded and influential, while the fight for disability rights by people with disabilities organisations seriously faltered, partly because of lack of funding, which reinforced their lack of influence. And while at that stage carers and people with disabilities groups were at war with each other over the issue of burden versus rights, services were relatively unchallenged and so were their models of care. However, the growing clamour from carers bore fruit.

'It is important to recognise that this push largely reflected carers' demands for services, as this meant that it was based on the vision for a significant expansion of disability services. The vision for the NDIS to be based on the strong principles of disability rights and citizenship came much later. There were the three vitally interested parties—carers, people with disabilities and service providers—all with different expectations of a solution.

'In the NPDCC, carers and people with disability networks really heard how it was from each other's point of view. People with disabilities were able to hear about how families did feel intolerably burdened, and carers were able to hear how much that term "burden" hurt people and also damaged the fight for rights.'

The very composition of the council as constructed by Shorten sought to heal these divisions: people were on it as individuals, not as representatives of any association. Further, the council included people from outside the disability sector as well, such as business and unions, to further inform the debate and spread the word.

John Della Bosca had seen the same dynamic at play during his time as the relevant New South Wales minister. 'The advocacy organisations, the service organisations and the carers organisations traditionally hadn't got on all that well. They tended to see one another as, if you like, almost the enemy, and the carers tended to be a bit standoffish with both advocates and providers, because oftentimes they would advocate in a way that people saw as a problem for families and carers. Anyway ... they didn't get along very well.'

Jan McLucas, too, had encountered this during her time as shadow minister, particularly while putting together the Senate report.

'You have people with disability; you have the carers of people with disability; and you also had the service sector, the service providers— and in that period 2004–07, there was not one voice amongst those three groups. There was a lot of friction between people with disability and the service sector. There was always friction between carers and the service sector. And the other thing that was happening then, the role of the carer—there was no intellectual basis there, there was no thought being put into what carers do. And a lot of the language around caring at that time was, "It's all about me", the carer, and it's all about how terrible my life is because I don't get any support from anybody.'

Disability advocate Sue Salthouse put the matter succinctly: 'People with disabilities, carers and disability organisations realised that we had to have a united voice if we were going to get anything.' All these divisions made it hard to effect change, because everyone's goals were different, their language was different, their strategy was different.

It helped, then, that an outsider, Shorten, arrived when he did. New to the scene, he was taken aback by the animosity between the groups. It was immediately clear to him that their capacity to get a message to government, let alone achieve an outcome, was drastically limited by the infighting.

Claire Moore, having sat on the Senate inquiry with Jan McLucas, recalls: 'Bill [Shorten] came in as parliamentary secretary for disabilities under the heading of "not the usual suspects", and I think that's very valuable because he brought in an independence of thought. And it came from not the social welfare side ... Jan [McLucas] and Jenny [Macklin] were very much in the social welfare area. And Bill came in and ... his response was, like, he didn't know about this stuff, and he wanted to know about this stuff, and he wanted to know why it hadn't been fixed ... He just gave it an energy, a different energy.'

Which is rather how Shorten remembers things too.

'What was happening up to that time was that the carers were concerned about the carers' particular issues, the blind people were only concerned with the blind, [those with] intellectual disabilities didn't want to be associated with the mentally ill and the people with mental illness would see them as another world. No one was sticking together. And that's why I wanted to come up with this idea of grassroots action.'

Bringing all the disparate groups, plus others, into this ministerial council meant they began to communicate and see each other's point of view. That did not mean they suddenly spoke with one voice—that moment would come later, as we shall see—but it did mean that they no longer spoke against each other. However, it didn't happen overnight, it didn't happen without pain, and it wouldn't be the end of the process.

Council member Nicole Lawder remembers the council's early days as fraught. 'It was, I think, a difficult time because it was one of the first times that people with disability and carers and service providers had come together. At times, especially in the start, it could get a bit heated. There were competing tensions in the meetings, and a bit of acrimony, and a bit of history to overcome. I think everyone had a genuine will to work well together. There might have been differences of opinion on particular issues. Bill [Shorten] was always very strong in emphasising that we all had to work together and there was also no doubting that the current systems were failing—no one argued with the fact that it was crap and something had to be done. Those tensions between the people with disability, carers and service providers continued, but we did, I think, reach a point where everyone knew what the goal was. There were differences, but Rhonda [Galbally] was a good chair.'

Another council member put it this way: 'Every time you get groups working together, there are some issues about who owns what and a sense of ownership and sense of power. Shorten finally said you can waste your time arguing about what you cannot agree on or focus on the 90 per cent on which you can agree.'

Yet another member concurs: 'It was a difficult time because it was one of the first times that people with disability and carers and service providers had come together, but we said, "This is what we want to achieve, this is where we need to get to." Under the guidance of Rhonda Galbally and her deputy chair, Kirsten Deane, who took charge along with Shorten, who attended at least the beginning of our sessions, largely to assist in direction setting—most people contributed and tried to work together ... We were beginning to actually contribute to the development of policy.'

With decades-long experience in the sector, Jenny Macklin knew the divisions as well as anyone. 'Historically, people with disability, carers and service providers had not been allies,' she explains. 'They'd often disagreed, and the disagreements had been fierce, but in what proved to be a critical decision, people with disability, carers and service providers decided to join together and create an alliance for change. Bill Shorten, my parliamentary secretary for disabilities, drawing on his union experience, was central to the establishment of the NPDC Council, with the people from all the different groups—people with disabilities, carers and service providers—coming together for the first time, with Rhonda Galbally as chair, and they were able to advocate strongly for disability reform. Bill proposed the very large membership of the ministerial council. It was a great decision.

'Bill was really shocked by the way people were being treated. A lot of credit goes to him. He really got out there and talked to people, advocating for change. He was the primary mover to set up DIG, which was looking at a whole range of options, and the Alliance [to come]. His message to the three groups—those with disability, the carers, the providers—was very clear: they have to come together. And Rhonda Galbally was critical. She was so important [in] getting the Alliance going, which was vital in getting out the message that things had to change.'

A key moment in Shorten's advocacy was a speech at the National Press Club in April 2009. He spoke of the couples whose marriages were falling apart due to the exhaustion of caring for a child with disability; of ageing parents haunted by the thought of who would care for their child after they died; of young adults living their lives in aged care because there was nowhere else for them. He said 500 000 people were primary carers for their loved ones—500 000 is the population of Tasmania. He spoke of the intellectually impaired in prison—1800 in New South Wales alone, over-represented by ten or twenty times their proportion of the general population. He spoke of those imprisoned in their own homes because of the unwillingness of others to employ them. He spoke of those imprisoned in their own shell because of the refusal of others to accept them.

Funds were a problem, he noted, but the first problem was lack of rights. 'To take a simple example: if someone was told they could not get on a bus, train or taxi because of their sex, or their old age, or the colour of their skin, there would be an outcry. If someone is unable to get on a bus because their wheelchair won't fit—we make no comment, we turn a blind eye,' he said. 'I think it's up to us, to all of us, to say: "This bus isn't moving until we're all on board."'

Cases concerning disability discrimination brought under Victoria's Equal Opportunity Act outnumbered those for sex, race, religion and colour *combined*. They accounted for more than half of cases taken to the Human Rights Commission.

The most systemic discrimination was in the workplace: being denied a job ensured poverty, and all that goes with it. 'Take this example of four people looking for work,' Shorten said. 'One, let's call him Leo, is deaf; the second, Frank, is in a wheelchair and the third, Helen, is blind, and the fourth, Steve, cannot make himself understood. It is likely that all four resumes would be put on the bottom of the pile by a boss or a job agency too concerned about the problems that these unhappy unfortunates might cause. That boss would have turned down Ludwig van Beethoven, Franklin D Roosevelt, Helen Keller and Stephen Hawking.'

Then he turned to the National Disability Insurance Scheme, on which he was awaiting a report.

'This is a big idea. It's as big as the original idea for Medibank [as Medicare was originally called]. It would turn our current system of providing disability services on its head. This proposed new approach would provide individualised lifetime care and support for each person from the point of diagnosis.

'Support should begin on the day a child's condition is diagnosed—which in many cases is before birth. Missing out on valuable learning early in life is a missed opportunity that can never be regained.

'Individual case managers would work with individuals and their families and carers, developing customised plans of treatment, care and support, aids and equipment, transport, home modifications and so on. For the first time there would be certainty and a whole-of-life perspective for people with disabilities and their families.

'It's a simple yet exciting and visionary idea.

'The extra money that we would need to achieve all this should not be seen by society as a cost. It should be seen as a valuable investment in creating adults who are able to work, be fulfilled and be independent.'

Shorten stressed people with disability wanted nothing special, just what others had. 'In all this, it is impossible to over-emphasise the need, the primal need, that people with disability feel, and it's the need to be ordinary, to not be thought of as amusing, or pitiable, or brave, or admirable, or coping wonderfully with difficult circumstances.'

In the end, it all came down to rights.

'I believe this is the last frontier of practical civil rights in this country.'

Bruce Bonyhady heard the speech. He could feel that things were changing. 'Bill was deeply committed and prepared to use his political power as a catalyst for change. In that address to the National Press Club he described the existing disability system as "broken" and that became a burning platform on which reform became inevitable. So, you've got a very active parliamentary secretary, you've got a very senior minister, deeply committed to the issue, you've got the Disability Investment Group doing some work, and also the National People with Disabilities and Carer Council working on the *Shut Out* report. It's all coming together.'

It is a law of the jungle that as resources dwindle, the fight for them intensifies. As we have seen, no one was being denied resources more than were those with disabilities—the consequence was that the fights for scraps left on the table was fierce.

This conflict resulted in a hidden consequence, one that the sector was unaware of, one that hurt it deeply. Being such a minefield of historic and ideological enmities, it became a minefield for politicians. If you helped one organisation, that meant there were ten, or twenty, or thirty other organisations that you did not help. By helping one, you earned the wrath of all the others. It is easy to be cynical about politicians and their motives, but it is smarter to examine the dynamics. The cynical view is that there were no votes in disability, and that is why funding the sector never seemed to be as high a priority as it should have been. But the smarter view reveals the hidden trap: it wasn't simply that there were no votes in it, but that there were *negative* votes in it, due to alienating all the other groups when giving help to one group.

Bonyhady puts it neatly: 'Whenever a group was successful, the other groups really hated them. So, governments could never get any political capital out of increased funding as it was always seen as divisive and favouring one group over another group at least as deserving. So, the upshot of that was that we had a deeply divided sector and totally inadequate funding.'

By gathering these groups under the one umbrella, this seemingly intractable dilemma was sewn up. It brings to mind Lyndon Johnson's quip about FBI boss J Edgar Hoover—better to have him inside the tent pissing out, than outside pissing in.

In October 2008 Macklin and Shorten revealed the first great task for the council. In short, it was to go out, listen to the people, and report back to the government. Macklin and Shorten released a discussion paper that was circulated to all and sundry, inviting comment at public consultations. The questions it asked were open-ended: tell us about any barriers you (or someone you care for or support) encounter that hinder your participation in life; what are the greatest barriers that people with a disability face in participating fully in life; and an invitation: what are your comments, thoughts or ideas?

Those consultations would take place nationwide, between late October and the end of November, with written submissions welcome from those who could not attend.

'We would like to hear from people with disability, their families and carers, the organisations which represent them, employers, trade unions, researchers, and anyone with an interest in creating a better Australia for people with disability,' Shorten announced.

The hearings would inform the composition of the National Disability Strategy, an election commitment that had come out of the Senate inquiry into CSTDA funding. 'The Strategy will set the direction of future disability policy in Australia and deliver real outcomes for people with disability, their families and carers. It will focus on caring needs, education, training, accessibility, employment, income and social inclusion,' Shorten said.

The announcement was accompanied by a sweetener—a one-off payment of $1400 for a single Disability Support Pensioner, $2100 for a couple. This was part of the Rudd government's spending package to give the economy the support it needed in the midst of the GFC—a dark cloud that touched every government program at the time, and every announcement. 'The Rudd government recognises that many people with disability face barriers in society, and are struggling with cost-of-living pressures during this time of global financial uncertainty,' he continued.

The Australian Federation of Disability Organisations would conduct the hearings in rural and remote areas. In the capital cities, they were run by the Department of Families, Housing, Community Services and Indigenous Affairs (FaHCSIA).

'It will be an important mechanism in ensuring the principles of the United Nations Convention on the Rights of Persons with Disabilities are integrated into policies and programs affecting people with disability, their families and carers,' Shorten said.

∽

In the midst of all this headiness—a national disability insurance scheme getting on the agenda at the Australia 2020 Summit, and the ministerial council's preparations for a national roadshow, giving them a direct input into policy—the sector received another shot of adrenaline: Australia ratified the United Nations Convention on the Rights of Persons with Disabilities (UNCRPD).

The boost that it provided, especially to those who had focused for years on establishing their rights, cannot be overestimated.

The Howard government had signed up to the convention on the day it opened for signatures in New York, 30 March 2007. In March 2008 Labor's attorney-general, Robert McClelland, wrote to the Joint Standing Committee on Treaties asking for prompt consideration of the convention, which was referred to it on 4 June. Two weeks later, the committee recommended to parliament that the treaty be ratified. The Rudd government did so at the first available opportunity, on 17 July 2008. It entered into force on 16 August 2008—thirty days after ratification. The process was as speedy as it could be.

'Australia recognises that persons with disability enjoy legal capacity on an equal basis with others in all aspects of life,' read the national declaration ratifying the convention. 'Australia recognises that every person with disability has a right to respect for his or her physical and mental integrity on an equal basis with others. Australia recognises the rights of persons with disability to liberty of movement, to freedom to choose their residence ... on an equal basis with others.'

These words were read out and cheered by disability organisations across the country. They might have sounded a lot like words that governments had said in the past, but the sheer fact that they were uttered while agreeing to be bound by a UN treaty gave them weight. And it gave those with disabilities hope, as well as some portion of pride. Perhaps most of all, it gave the sector momentum—and momentum counts for an awful lot in politics.

Sue Salthouse, who was chair and then president of Women With Disabilities Australia, remembered it well. 'It was fantastic,' she recalled several years ago. 'We were so energised by the signing and ratification of the CRPD. That was such a unifying moment for us as well. So, there were celebrations, state by state and organisation by organisation,' she said, adding that it gave the sector overall a little more confidence in government.

Senator Claire Moore observed that the ratification had a uniting effect on the divided sector. 'This tended to bind the three sub-groups into a united purpose,' she said.

The convention's declared purpose was 'to promote, protect and ensure the full and equal enjoyment of all human rights and fundamental freedoms by all persons with disabilities, and to promote respect for their inherent dignity'.

It enumerated its general principles: respect, non-discrimination, full inclusion and participation in society, including equality of opportunity, for both sexes and for children. It bound its signatories to eliminate discrimination in marriage, education, health, employment, standards of living, and participation in political and public life.

The general obligations of countries signing up were to do what they could via legislation, policy and administration to ensure these rights, and to promote and develop universally designed goods, services, equipment and facilities to ensure these rights. 'Universally designed' means designed in such a way as not to be exclusive—to be accessible and usable by all. Countries were bound to use their resources to achieve these rights, and, in doing so, to consult with those with disabilities. Governments also agreed to raise awareness of disability, and ensure that education, transport, the built environment, information services and communications technology presented no obstacles to their use.

In short, the convention's twenty-eight pages were exhaustive as to what signatory countries were meant to do.

'Supporting the Convention is part of the Rudd government's commitment to ensuring that people with disabilities are not subject to treatment like they are second-class citizens,' Shorten said on the day.

The sense of optimism felt throughout the sector was reflected in the words of Australia's disability discrimination commissioner, Graeme Innes, speaking to parliament's Joint Standing Committee on Treaties in the immediate aftermath of ratification.

'Australia is among the first nations to ratify the convention,' he said. 'We are the thirtieth country to ratify, perhaps a record in ratifications, and more remarkable because of the complexities of our federal system in the ratification process. I commend the government for moving swiftly to ratify the convention.'

The entire ratification process requires considerable legwork behind the scenes; mostly invisible to observers, let alone the general public. Before negotiations even begin, the relevant minister needs a mandate from the minister of foreign affairs. The prime minister and any other relevant minister need to be informed. Lead agencies have to consult with the relevant government agencies and state governments, after which approval is needed from the Federal Executive Council (all ministers plus the governor-general), after which comes scrutiny by parliament via the Joint Standing Committee on Treaties.

'I would also like to recognise the previous government and their strong support of the convention,' Innes continued, 'which included signing it on the first day it was open for signature and playing an important and positive role during the drafting process in partnership with disability

community organisations. Early ratification has provided Australia with
the opportunity to participate in the development of the first treaty body
to operate under the convention. As a world leader in the development of
legislation, policy and services for people with disability, we have much to
contribute to such a body.'

The ratification had been prioritised at the urging of Shorten, partly
so that Australia could get a seat at the table at the United Nations.
Speed paid off: University of Sydney professor Ron McCallum was
appointed to the UN committee overseeing implementation of the convention, becoming its chairman in February 2010.

To be sure, the treaty did not become law in Australia—that's not
quite how such treaties work—but it did have legal effects. First and
foremost, Australia had agreed to be bound by the treaty. It meant that
other Australian laws—such as anti-discrimination legislation, disability
services legislation, guardianship laws and even the CSTDA funding
agreements—had to be in compliance with it. That opened up the
possibility of the Human Rights Commission auditing laws to ensure
compliance with the treaty, as recommended by the joint standing committee. Legislation was, in fact, audited to make sure it did comply.

Signing up was much more than symbolic—but its symbolic value
was immense.

The treaty also came with a so-called 'Optional Protocol'. It gave individuals the right to take a case to the UN Committee on the Rights of
Persons with Disabilities if that person believed Australia was not in compliance with the treaty, and if they had exhausted all legal avenues here.

On 28 July Philip Lynch, the then director and principal solicitor
of the Human Rights Law Centre in Melbourne, addressed the joint
standing committee, and urged Australia to sign up to the Optional
Protocol as well. 'It would seem incongruous if Australia was not to
accept the jurisdiction of the [UN] disability committee over individual

complaints. Indeed, it would place disability rights on a lower level than women's rights, rights of particular racial and religious minorities, and so on. I think ratification of the OP therefore has a very important symbolic role to play, in addition obviously to the very important role it will play in providing effective remedies.' The committee acceded, and Australia duly signed up to the Optional Protocol as well.

As significant a moment as this was, though, it was not going to change the world overnight.

As Commissioner Innes said to the joint standing committee, 'Ratification is not the conclusion of the process of recognising human rights for people with disabilities. In Australia we have made some great advances in disability law and policy, but there is much more to do. We must strive to remove barriers to physical and information access; ensure equal opportunity, not just in theory but in practice, in employment and education; and address the severe inadequacies in supports and services for many people with disability and their families. Ratification of the convention is a symbolic commitment to equal enjoyment of human rights for Australians with disability. I now urge all Australian governments to work together and in partnership with the community to make that commitment a reality.'

Ratifying the convention gave many disability advocates what they had long searched for: a basis in law, a foundation in rights, on which they could stake their claims, beyond domestic legislation. It was precisely this lack of rights that had engendered the begging-bowl approach: all you could ever do was ask for help when you had no legal instrument to use to enforce a claim, or no legal foundation on which to base a claim. In that sense, the convention brought a degree of certainty, a form of guarantee, that these rights were something more than abstract principles and were extant legalities that had force; that these rights could not be withdrawn on a whim; that they were not extinguishable simply because the money had run out. These rights now had to be taken into consideration at every step of the way. The convention was one more plank in the construction of a better world.

∽

In the eight capital cities of Australia's states and territories, the *Shut Out* hearings spanned October and November 2008 and were attended by thousands of people, with hundreds and hundreds of submissions, and many of the hearings chaired by Rhonda Galbally.

In regional and rural Australia, the hearings were even more numerous, taking place in forty separate locations, from dusty Fitzroy Crossing in the remote Kimberley, 2500 kilometres from Perth, with a population at the time of not quite 1000; to verdant Sale, Victoria, diagonally opposite in the south-east corner of the continent. There was the testimony of people in sleepy Cobram, whose 5000 residents were nestled on the Murray River; and people told their stories 2500 kilometres away from there, in tropical Cairns. The 4500 citizens of Condobolin, 450 kilometres west of Sydney, sitting on the Macquarie River, got to speak as well; as did the people of Bunbury, all the way over on the Indian Ocean, four days' drive away. Many of those speaking, especially in places distant from where the big decisions get made, felt that they were being heard for the first time. This was not the public consultation that people feared—a charade giving them five minutes in the spotlight to vent, feel better, and then go back to a life of being ignored. This was something altogether different.

The floor was open to everyone: those with disabilities, their parents, their carers; representatives of the disabilities service sector; business-people; lobby groups, advocates and activists; non-government agencies, government officials, be they local, state or national—to name just a few.

The aim of the hearings was clear and succinct: to hear from those involved what the barriers in their lives were. What the barriers were that prevented them from living lives as full and meaningful as they could be. Further, what would help to remove those barriers.

It was an opportunity to speak—and, likewise, an opportunity to listen. Politics is an art, a game, a craft. Its ways can be mysterious, bathed in the shadows of backroom deals, or it can be a naked gladiatorial contest, fought in the public domain, visible to all. The skills it demands are numerous and often contradictory; you must be a people pleaser, but to be any good, you must also be prepared to make the hard decisions. You must be able to make allies, but also to detect and defeat enemies. A lot of it is tricky stuff, with your enemies—not just in the opposing party but, more pertinently, in your own party—keen to jump on your errors, and the media more than happy to go along for the ride. But sometimes, just sometimes, politics is very, very simple. Sometimes the most important thing to do is to listen. As they say, you learn while you're listening, not while you're talking. When Shorten was made parliamentary secretary for disabilities after the 2007 election, he realised the first thing he had to do was listen. To find out how this thing worked—or didn't work. To hear people's stories. What he thought after listening was that the nation needed to hear this story too.

The first hearing took place in Darwin on 27 October 2008, attended by a modest twenty people. By the time the last hearing was held, in Geelong six weeks later, the landscape had changed. Anyone paying even the slightest attention knew that the country had a problem that needed to be fixed.

The extraordinarily high degree of public participation in the hearings spoke to the great suffering imposed on all those involved—first and foremost those with disabilities, and their families.

Many stood, if they could, to tell their story—of the difficulties they faced, of the torments they endured, of the discrimination they suffered. They bared their souls in public, in front of strangers, to get their stories out.

One part of the message getting through was that it was not simply the disability that was the problem but, rather, everything else. As one person put it: 'It is society which handicaps me, far more seriously and completely than the fact that I have spina bifida.' For those who had never given the topic a thought—which is to say, many millions of people—it was obvious that being restricted to a wheelchair makes life difficult; the necessary mental leap was to give a moment's thought to the fact that the steps at the entrance to a museum, or an art gallery, or Parliament House, keep that person out, whereas a ramp will let them in. Then you see that the barrier is not the disability, the rest of the world is.

The essential thing was to get this conversation started, and the hearings were doing that. Political change, social change, does not happen overnight: it is a long process, which requires volume and repetition, stories and repetition, data and repetition, agitation and repetition, advocacy and repetition, listening and repetition. Only at the point when there is a generalised and consensual notion that we have a problem does the government of the day have the confidence it needs in order to believe it has the imprimatur for change. The process—in getting the problem out into the light of day, as opposed to being hidden behind locked doors, people in their private pain—was beginning.

For so long, those with disabilities had been invisible and voiceless, unseen and unheard, living in a hidden city, as Shorten phrased it. Here, however, was a platform—not merely for grandstanding, but as a launching pad for change. Once Australians heard these stories, they could no longer live in ignorance; no longer ignore a problem they did not see, that they had not heard about. Once these stories were heard, there was no unhearing them. That, indeed, was the intention.

'I knew that there was no turning back for our government. These problems, once identified, would have to be fixed,' Macklin said.

A grand total of 332 organisations made submissions, from the Ability Employment Group to the Youth Disability Advocacy Service; from local councils to state ombudsmen; from professional bodies representing psychologists, physiotherapists, engineers and so on, to professional bodies representing business, such as Clubs Australia, and unions, represented by the ACTU. Advocacy groups, be they representing the deaf, the blind, the autistic, the intellectually impaired, those with Down syndrome and so on, did not miss the opportunity to speak. Their very number spoke to the myriad ways in which the people they represented intersected with everyone and everything else—and the difficulties that entailed. It also spoke, in a more subtle way, to the fractured system, to the incoherent and uncoordinated way in which their problems were approached by governments of all levels.

Private individuals made even more submissions—about 440 all up. In excess of 2500 people attended the hearings, either supporting those speaking or to hear their tales for themselves. That huge response was indicative of an underlying but overwhelming need for change; it spoke to the unbearable conditions under which people were forced to live, not simply because of their disabilities, but the inability of the rest of the world to accommodate them. One recurring theme was how government policies often worked against those they were designed to help.

Once the hearings were over and it was time to examine what people had said, very clear patterns emerged. More than half the participants said that social exclusion was a major barrier for them, as was accessing the very services that were provided.

About one third nominated insufficient income, especially given the extra costs associated with disability, as a barrier to a full life. As we know, higher income levels often derive from higher education—almost the same percentage, one third, said that problems getting an education were a major barrier. The same percentage said that problems finding a job were a major barrier.

The same proportion said that a lack of formal rights in any of the legislation was a major hindrance to leading a normal life.

Almost a third of the participants pointed to the difficulties in using transport—getting a bus or a tram, or a train or a plane—as a barrier, keeping them locked up indoors rather than being out in the world. It was the same with getting access to health care.

The plentiful stories were sad, maddening—sometimes shocking.

One young man was denied a vital organ transplant because of his disability—but was invited to become a donor. This submission said, 'We can put men on the moon ... but we cannot fulfil basic needs enabling our disabled community to live with human dignity.'

Education emerged as a major issue. Australians have long since become accustomed to the fact that education is a right—but it's not so for children with disabilities. One third of submissions were about the lack of available education. Children with disabilities were routinely excluded from kindergartens and schools. Schools were not equipped; teachers were not trained. The frustration this created for parents, who felt they were failing their children, was immense. The stats bore out the problem: by this time, more than 80 per cent of people were progressing past Year 10 but only half of those with disability did so.

The problems with schools started with children with disabilities not being admitted in the first place, but they hardly ended there. Many complained about teachers who were unwilling or unable to help—which raised questions about whether teachers had received any relevant training. One person with a hearing disability recounted how their Year 8 science teacher refused to wear her mic because it supposedly put holes in her clothes. The student failed science that year—and topped the science class the next year, when a different teacher happily wore the mic.

One parent recounted being told that their child would not be going on excursions because the school would not pay the extra money to hire a bus with wheelchair access.

The pain of parents who felt they could not entrust their children to schools because of a lack of understanding on the behalf of teachers was all too evident.

Teachers, too, were frustrated, especially in situations when they could see a child needed extra support that was not being provided.

Not being able to exercise the right to give a child an education at a school of choice—denominational, independent or state—was another limitation encountered by many.

As well, the social exclusion experienced by many children with disabilities at school too often was only a precursor to that later in life. One woman told how the requirements of the Home and Community Care Program meant she had to ask her housemates to move out as her level of assistance depended on the income of co-residents—who were only housemates, not carers, not family. The end result was isolation and loneliness—the cumulative outcome for many, thanks to the multiple exclusions and barriers they faced on a lifelong basis.

One mother reported the experience of taking her intellectually disabled daughter to gym classes. 'The gym offered a separate class for kids with disabilities,' she said. 'I asked one of the teachers whether it would be possible for my daughter to attend one of the other mainstream classes. She frowned and looked concerned, and said that was why they had created the separate class. I said she was perfectly capable of joining in with the other girls. She said, "Well, that's OK for your daughter but if we let her in we will have to let everyone else in." These are not elite gymnasts. They are little girls jumping around in leotards having fun on a Saturday morning.'

One revealing statistic was that almost 15 per cent of people with disabilities lived alone, which was more than double the rate for the non-disabled population. The inability to do normal things thus compounded that isolation. Many of those in shared accommodation reported that they interacted with no one other than their housemates and their carers.

Many of those carers were family members—and many of them were, likewise, living a life of isolation, lonely, depressed and poor, as they struggled to do all they could for loved ones.

Problems with housing were raised again and again—in almost one in three submissions. Many reported being unable to get the necessary support to live independently. Many parents, too, complained that their children wanted to live independently—and they wanted to see their children achieve their independence—but could not, because such housing wasn't available or wasn't suitable.

The fact remained that people with disability had no choice who they lived with in shared accommodation. That could be unpleasant or uncomfortable, but it could also be much worse—unsafe. One mother reported complaining that her son was being sexually abused by another man at his group home, only to be told that nothing could be done—no other accommodation was available. A woman with a physical disability shared a house with two men and, after being struck by one of them, felt unsafe.

The issue of ageing parents—some in their eighties and nineties—caring for their children at home was raised again and again. Their anguish at not being able to get supported accommodation for their children was all too palpable. More than one submission related the fact that it was still the case that really desperate parents resorted to simply abandoning their children while in care, to solve the problem. One person assessed that state of affairs this way: 'Governments rely on most parents never being able to bring themselves to abandon their children. Deep parental love and a sense of duty are being deliberately exploited solely in order to save money, which in a country as wealthy as Australia is profoundly shocking. But even the most devoted and self-sacrificing of parents can't keep on caring if they're dead.'

Health care was yet another recurring issue. People repeatedly said they could not receive the everyday medical services that the rest of the population could so easily obtain. A particularly shocking instance was the case of a woman born with motor neurone disease. After her mother died, she moved into a nursing home, and from there into independent living, where she lived by herself. She was very active, starting up a social group for young people living in nursing homes. On the eve of a house-warming party, she became ill. Not having had yearly health check-ups, she had developed kidney stones, which she had not detected herself, having no feeling from the waist down. After being denied help from the after-hours disability service, she called an ambulance, was admitted into intensive care and placed in an induced coma. She never returned home. She died five months later, in hospital.

So many of those with disability were forced to live in poverty, which has so many causes. Being denied a proper education was a root cause. Being discriminated against in the employment market was another. Being restricted in movement likewise limited the available jobs. Lacking necessary supports was yet another impediment to gaining a good income. Another terrible case was heard, of a 45-year-old woman who had lost most of her vision because of type 2 diabetes. Losing her vision meant she lost her job—her employer would not provide any changes in the workplace, or give her time off to learn how to use various assistive technologies. Now unemployed, stressed and anxious, she was trying to negotiate the social security system, but finding it all but impossible, due to her lack of vision.

Employment statistics bore out the inequality—labour participation was 53 per cent, compared with 81 per cent for people without disabilities. Drilling down, the situation was worse, for 'labour participation' includes those looking for work, not just those with a job. Vision Australia figures showed that 63 per cent of people who were blind or vision impaired were underemployed or unemployed.

On top of all the limiting factors in relation to income, the cost of living was far higher for those with a disability. Many aids were extremely expensive—up to $10 000 for a wheelchair, and a similar cost for hearing aids—and many were forced to buy these themselves on the private market if they were deemed ineligible; or the waiting lists were too long; or if they were eligible but, sorry, the money has run out. Waiting lists could be so long that a child would have outgrown the approved wheelchair by the time it was delivered.

The difficulty in obtaining these assistive technologies was another oft-mentioned problem. One submission demonstrated how this restricted participation in public life by making it difficult to vote. This person was a 45-year-old woman living in rural Australia. She had a political science degree and a deep interest in civic life. Yet, until 2007 she had been unable to cast her own vote—which implies her ballot was not secret—because she was blind. She had to rely on others—carers, friends, electoral officials—to help her vote. At the 2007 election, she made a six-hour, 200-kilometre round trip simply so she could cast her own vote, thanks to the technology available at that particular polling booth.

The UNCRPD would help this woman and all other people in her situation. Under its provision to enable everyone to participate in public life, there was an obligation to protect 'the right of persons with disabilities to vote by secret ballot in elections and public referendums ... facilitating the use of assistive and new technologies where appropriate'. No such right had existed here; now it did.

Problems compounded other problems. One family reported they needed a hoist to lift their son in and out of bed. They may well have been eligible for a hoist—but first an occupational therapist had to make an assessment. The waiting list to have an occupational therapist make such an assessment was eighteen months.

If that seems like an awful bureaucratic bind to be caught in, the system was capable of throwing up even weirder things. Consider the case of one girl who did receive the communication device her family had requested. Her mother inquired: 'Why does my daughter have a communication device that talks in a male American computerised voice? Why can't she have a communication device that has a voice of a young Australian girl?' Is it dignified for an Australian girl to be forced to sound like an American man?

About one in five submissions referenced the difficulty in obtaining the aids that could ensure full participation in life. As one person put it plainly: 'There is much talk of community involvement and participation, but when individuals don't have access to the necessary mobility and communication tools to partake, then it is not possible.'

Those appearing at the hearings also pointed to the problems with access. The difficulties of getting into a building were one thing, but the problems did not stop at the front door. Lack of accessible bathrooms can be as great a barrier as a flight of stairs at the main entrance. Likewise, the lack of braille in a lift is a deterrent, and increases dependency. Uneven or reflective surfaces can also make life difficult.

The exclusions were everywhere, and people pointed out they were not asking for anything special. As one put it: 'I do not expect to get access to the pyramids or Uluru, but I do want to get into all of the library and all of the community centre.'

Many—almost one third—spoke of how they felt trapped and excluded by public transport, including taxis. The main problem was access, but there were also the staff who refused to provide the help they were meant to, and a lack of safety on public transport. Some noted that things were improving with regard to accessibility, but slowly. In 2002 the Howard government passed a law mandating that all of Australia's public transport networks, except trams and trains, be fully accessible by the end of 2022. Trains and trams have until 2032.

Indigenous Australians faced multiple layers of disadvantage, starting with the scarcity, or non-existence, of supports in remote areas. That often necessitated moving house, an expense in itself that may come with consequences for Indigenous Australians it wouldn't for others. Cultural misunderstandings, such as regarding the composition of Indigenous families and the notion of 'shared care', also complicated matters. The difficulty of making Indigenous Australians aware of what services were available made things even worse, as it did for those Australians for whom English was not their first language.

Beyond the personal stories of lived experience, many submissions reflected on the service system they were living in; the system designed to help them. Many reported that it, instead, hindered them—once they had jumped the many hurdles in accessing services in the first place.

The general picture that emerged from the many voices was that the system was broken—chronically underfunded and under resourced, with services that were unavailable, inappropriate and infrequent. It was a system driven by the crises of those within it, which had thrown the system itself into a state of permanent crisis.

One repeated complaint was that a person was expected to fit into the system, rather than it responding to the needs of the people it was servicing. Services were what they were, with little choice or flexibility. Services did not adapt to changes in life and changes in need. The system denied users any sense of agency, denied them the feeling of even being a person. The fact of having to apply for support could in itself make people feel like beggars; the process was spirit crushing when applications failed. Spirit crushing sometimes even when they succeeded—if, say, the communication device or hoist had been approved, but would not arrive for eighteen months.

To rub salt into the wound, as many pointed out, people with disabilities were often seen as a burden on society—as charity cases, who should be grateful for whatever they received. And, of course, they could not do the simple things that others take for granted. 'In this day and age, imagine if a person was told that they could only go to ten cinemas in Australia and to one of three sessions a week because of their gender, cultural background or religious beliefs. But as a deaf person, that is what I face. I am very limited in where I can go and when, to access things that other people take for granted,' said one person.

Individualised services were a desiderata for many, as was the capacity to choose your own services. The desire for independence was raised many times, not just in relation to living independently but in being allowed to make *any* decisions for yourself.

Funding was identified over and over again as the root cause of so many other problems—the disability system simply was not funded to the point where it met demand. There were various suggestions as to how funding, or the funding process, could be improved. One stood out—a national disability insurance scheme, akin to Medicare, to provide lifelong support.

~

The evidence and testimony, the stories and anecdotes, the tears and fears, the pleas and ideas that were heard and read by all the many hundreds of people and organisations who contributed to the public consultation were gathered into the report *Shut Out*.

It was launched in August 2009 by Jenny Macklin. 'To turn a good policy idea into a major reform, you have to build the case for change,' she later recalled. 'With the NDIS, we built the case on a variety of fronts. The disability sector spelled out the full extent of the problem, producing the *Shut Out* report. It painted a terrible picture of a failed system. When I launched the *Shut Out* report, I knew that there was no turning back for our government.'

She recalls that launch fondly and proudly—and maybe with a bit of a shudder, at the high-wire act she was now engaged in.

'I remember the day we launched the *Shut Out* report and thinking, *My goodness, it says just how bad things are*. I couldn't launch this thing and then not do anything.' But it was a long way from being clear what would be done—by this stage, there was a determination there be an NDIS, but so many questions remained unanswered, including the main one, funding.

'There was a concerted series of actions in organising a broad coalition of allies,' says Shorten. 'Get together an economic investment team, which links us into the business community; build up a community base, which was via the ministerial advisory council, and then you need the drum beat of educating people on the problem—and that was *Shut Out*. I would have done a hundred meetings around the country talking about the NDIS. We were headed towards building a broad-based community grass-roots organisation, which became the Every Australian Counts campaign, to keep explaining to people what the problem was, and *Shut Out* was one step in that process.'

The primary author of *Shut Out* was Kirsten Deane, who recalls that bureaucrats had advised Macklin not to release it—that the report painted too grim a picture, which left the government exposed. Galbally says that the council members contributed to the report, with Helen Hambling, who also worked on DIG, having input.

'Jenny went ahead and released it. It was very brave,' Deane says. 'Frankly, it was very brave of the commonwealth to put it out, you know; it could have just been a report from the council. But it got put out as a commonwealth government report, with the commonwealth logo on it. And we wanted it to be stark—it came out with a black cover and yellow writing. It wasn't called, you know, a report about their consultations for the National Disability Strategy. It was called *Shut Out*. It is as advertised on the box. So it was a very unusual report. It reflected very well on the commonwealth at the time, both the minister and the department, that they put it out in the way they did. It wasn't your average report.'

The title, *Shut Out*, referenced the lived experience of deinstitutionalisation—whereas once those with disabilities had been shut inside the forbidding walls of institutions, now they were shut out of society. Once they were segregated; now they were isolated. People with disabilities were in the community, but not part of the community.

In her capacity as chair of the council, Galbally had attended every sitting in the capital cities. It may have given some of those making their submissions heart that she came and went in her wheelchair, the result of a childhood case of polio, like so many children of the 1950s. Thanks to school vaccinations, the fear of polio is something we longer have to endure.

'What I heard was both intensely moving and profoundly shocking,' Galbally wrote in her preface to *Shut Out*. 'We live in one of the wealthiest countries in the world and yet all too often people with disabilities struggle to access the very necessities of life—somewhere to live, somewhere to work. All too often they are unable to access education, health care, recreation and sport—the very things most people in the community take for granted. They are denied access to kindergartens, schools, shopping centres and participation in community groups. They are often isolated and alone. Their lives are a constant struggle for resources and support.

'Aboriginal and Torres Strait Islanders with disabilities face a particular battle. They experience the dual disadvantage of prejudice because of their disability and racism because of their heritage. Disability services rarely understand their cultural needs, while mainstream services rarely understand the nature and experience of disability.'

She noted the fact that disability can strike anyone, anywhere, at any time—the importance of which would become clearer and clearer in the coming years and be a significant factor in how the case for the NDIS was argued.

'Many people in the community believe disability is someone else's problem. They do not believe disability will touch their lives, and give little thought to the experience of living with disability, or caring for someone with a disability. Without first-hand experience, they hold on to the belief that at least things are better than they used to be.

'The stories you will find in this report will challenge those beliefs.

'As this report sadly illustrates, Australians with disabilities are among our nation's forgotten people. But it is time for their stories to be heard—and acted upon.

'I came away from those consultations both angry and sad. But most of all, I came away determined. Australians with disabilities have been waiting for many years for change. They cannot and will not wait any longer.'

Her sentiments were echoed in a foreword co-signed by Macklin and Shorten.

'Many Australians with disabilities, along with their families, friends and carers, are still experiencing systemic disadvantage. The national ideal of a "fair go" is still only imperfectly extended to people with disabilities,' they wrote.

'The people who participated are, just like all other Australian citizens, individuals with their own needs, abilities, ambitions and priorities. They are united only by the experience of living with disability.

'Yet a consistent message from their contributions is the desire to have the same opportunities as everyone else for a fulfilling and productive life. Many said they face a constant struggle to obtain what the rest of the community would consider to be an ordinary life. They do not want special treatment—they just want the barriers removed so they can get on with living.'

The argument that people with disabilities did not want anything special really had an effect. People came to see that their case was not one of special pleading. It was simply the desire to start on an equal footing. It was the theme that Shorten had raised in his speech to the National Press Club—the right to an ordinary life.

This was put eloquently in one submission, and highlighted in the report: 'We desire a place within the community! This place is not just somewhere to lay down our heads, but a place which brings comfort and support with daily living, friendship, meaningful work, exciting recreation, spiritual renewal, relationships in which we can be ourselves freely with others. And out of this great things may flourish.

'Perhaps we will begin to feel better about ourselves, to come to know ourselves as honoured, respected, accepted, yes, loved. To be healed from shame, feeling unworthy, undesirable, ugly, difficult, not smart enough, not sporty enough, not lovely enough. And perhaps we might be freed from our terrible daily fears that it all won't last, that more rejection is written into our lives. Maybe our dreams will no longer be filled with the traumatic fear of others pushing us around.

'Perhaps a time will come when we no longer have to protect ourselves from loss and can feel that this place is the place of creation, of re-creation, co-creation. Perhaps then our loneliness will fade. Perhaps then we will belong and our gifts (perhaps meagre, perhaps spectacular) freely shared. And from there will flow all the delights and tragedies of a life lived in the community, shaped not by exclusion and oppression but by everyday ordinariness.'

People with disabilities had been freed from incarceration in remote institutions, out of sight and out of mind; now they had to be freed from the private homes, the shared accommodation, the group houses, the cluster housing in which they were caged because the outside world—the schools, the workplaces, the transport systems, the cinemas, cafes and football grounds—still failed to accommodate them.

'The task that falls to us,' Macklin and Shorten continued, 'is to make the political, social and economic changes necessary to enable this to happen. We have been told we need to tackle issues and barriers around disability services, we need to ensure an adequate standard of living for all our citizens, and we need a society in which all people are included and are supported as citizens and leaders in the community.'

◡

While working on the *Shut Out* report, Kirsten Deane felt the necessity of doing justice to the stories people told—in particular, the intensity of the needs and the anguish of them not being met.

'Because of everything that we had seen and heard, the effort people had made, I just felt this enormous sense of responsibility to tell the stories the way they had been told, as part of the consultations. I didn't want to tell it in an anodyne government way, but tell it in a way that was true to the honesty and the rawness and the courage and the generosity that people had given in sharing their stories. And I wanted to be true to that, and tell it in a way that would resonate with people who didn't have any experience of it.'

Deane agrees with Macklin's observations that making known the circumstances in which people with disabilities lived, exposing the difficulties in their lives, would catalyse action by jogging the conscience of the country.

'Yes, that's exactly what I always used to say about it. Unless you were a person with a disability, a family member or a friend, pre NDIS, I think that people's vision of Australia is that we have some semblance of a social safety net and that the bad old days of institutions are gone. People thought, *We're Australia, we're a progressive country, surely we look after people with disability; I can't believe that we wouldn't.* Unless you had personal experience, I think that average members of the Australian public had no idea that people with disability who needed personal care would only get one or two showers a week.

'I think they had no idea that families would have to mortgage their homes to pay for support for their children. I think they had no idea, as was our experience, that local schools would turn away children with disability. I think people just had no idea. And once you said to people, "This is the problem. This is what happens every single day—children are turned away from schools, kids don't get the early intervention they need to really reach their full potential. Families are struggling.

This is what life is like every single day for so many people in this country"—well, they get it then. We were nudging the public along. People just didn't know. And *Shut Out* was one step in getting them to know.'

Deane recalls attending one hearing and sitting on the platform. 'I identify with people with disability and their families. This is my community. I do remember at least one of them that I attended. I had to work really hard to keep myself together, because we were up on a stage, and I remember that feeling of sitting there going, *It's probably not going to be really cool if I cry*. I just went home and cried afterwards—the stories that you heard, it was so hard.'

Deane points out that it is quite unusual for government hearings such as these to attract more submissions from private individuals than from organisations, which usually predominate. The process had mobilised the sector. It had engendered momentum, which would not stop.

The process had thus served its purpose—or, rather, its multiple purposes. By platforming the voices of those with disabilities, it had started bringing to the surface of the national consciousness just how unnecessarily difficult their lives were. These insights were incorporated into framing the National Disability Strategy then being formulated.

Further, the work of the 28-member council in formulating the process had brought them into the one room, sitting around the same table. In doing so, their commonalities had started to emerge, resolving, to some degree, their differences in outlook, philosophy and strategy—a consequence of the process not necessarily visible at the outset, but vital when considered in hindsight.

That unity began to change the conversation, both within and outside the disability sector. 'The burden discourse began to abate,' Rhonda Galbally recalls, 'although I do have to admit that without it, we might not have won the hearts and minds of the community and the politicians. However, the tension implicit in these different views of people with disabilities—as people to be cared for, or as people where supports can mean that they can care for themselves—is crucial to understand and keep in mind.'

'People with disabilities want to bring about a transformation of their lives,' *Shut Out* stated. 'They want their human rights recognised and realised. They want the things that everyone else in the community takes for granted. They want somewhere to live, a job, better health care, a good education, a chance to enjoy the company of friends and family, to go to the footy and to go to the movies. They want the chance to participate meaningfully in the life of the community. And they are hopeful. They desire change and they want others in the community to share their vision. They recognise that governments cannot work in isolation, and they want others to see the benefits of building more inclusive communities.'

We see here the argument subtly morphing, in two ways. The rights argument was coming to predominate, bolstered and bulwarked by the fact that the rights were now enshrined in the United Nations Convention. Further, the demand was simple: *we want a life*.

'We were one of the first countries,' the ministerial foreword continued, 'to ratify the United Nations Convention on the Rights of Persons with Disabilities as part of the Australian Government's broader long-term commitment to improving the lives of people with disabilities, their families, friends and carers.' The government was using the convention as a tool to make itself comply.

The hearings had established the case for change, making it clear to the community that a very large proportion of the population was not getting a fair go. *Shut Out* took that one step further: in response to those voices, it suggested the changes that needed to be made. These would now be incorporated into the National Disability Strategy. That had been a promise made in the 2007 federal election campaign—the vow to examine how to finance, fund and deliver disability services, which now had a deadline attached: mid-2010.

In the end, however, it all came down to one simple proposition, as stated modestly by Macklin and Shorten: 'The sentiments expressed in this submission—the right to be treated with dignity and to have the same opportunities as other members of the Australian community—should not be too much to ask.'

Put that way, the proposition was impossible to argue against. As the case came before the Australian people, they would agree.

⌇

Many of those involved at the senior levels, and many others throughout the sector, were aware by now, either dimly or in a focused fashion, of the idea for a national scheme to fund disability. They might have been aware of it from the time it had been mentioned in two submissions to the Senate inquiry in 2006–07. They were probably aware of it surfacing at the 2020 summit, and then again, a month later, when the summit self-reported. They were reminded of it a year later, by the government response to the summit, which recommended further consideration of the idea. They were aware of it again thanks to the idea being raised in submissions to *Shut Out*. Those with long-enough memories might have recalled vaguely that the Whitlam government had wanted to do something along these lines in the 1970s. Those with a historical bent might have been aware of the efforts in the 1920s, 1930s and 1940s.

The idea was seeping into other areas of policy development. The Pension Review, commissioned by Macklin to strengthen the financial security of age pensioners and those on the Disability Support Pension (DSP), reported in February 2009 and had as one of its findings that an NDIS was 'worthy of further consideration'. The review, which was coordinated with the Henry Tax Review, had an advisory council, on which

Bruce Bonyhady sat. It was chaired by Jeff Harmer—who, you will recall, had been introduced to the idea of the NDIS before the 2007 election by Bonyhady and John Walsh. Macklin recalls, 'The point I made to Jeff was "It's fantastic what you are doing with the DSP, but if you have a severe and permanent disability, the costs you experience are much higher than the population as a whole, so we need an NDIS alongside the pension."'

The Pension Review noted that the notion was being explored elsewhere within government. Pieces of the jigsaw were coming together.

In April 2009 the House of Representatives Standing Committee on Family, Community, Housing and Youth received the *Who Cares?* report. It inquired into ensuring better support for carers, and also referenced the NDIS.

MS Australia submitted that an NDIS 'is a necessity for Australia's health system from both a financing and service delivery perspective'. A private individual's submission pointed to such schemes covering those who had been in work and car accidents in various states, noting also the control, choice and confidence it would confer on those with disabilities and their carers. The report anticipated further research elsewhere, and concluded that the system might need 'a new and innovative approach'—and that an NDIS might be that approach.

More funds were needed; everyone knew that, even though the amounts dedicated were already immense. But more funds alone, it was clear by now, would not be enough—the system still had to be reoriented towards the individual. No amount of reorientation would or could do the job by itself—there had to be more funds.

At the National Press Club on 7 October 2009, Rhonda Galbally, speaking in the wake of *Shut Out*, made a stirring case for the National Disability Insurance Scheme.

Pointing to the failure of the system, she said that carrying on business as usual would be 'both socially and financially irresponsible—even scandalous'.

The safety net was broken. A new one was needed. The NDIS.

'A National Disability Insurance Scheme would provide funding for early intervention, essential care, support, therapy, aids and equipment, home modifications and training,' she said, her tone measured.

'Most importantly, it would provide this early on in order to maximise potential, facilitate independence and ensure planned transitions over the life course. The scheme would, in short, provide people with what they need, when they need it, to ensure they reach their full potential.'

Her argument was based on rights and equity.

'It will put an end to the current inequities that see people receiving different levels of support depending on how their disability is acquired.

'It shouldn't matter whether you are born with a disability, acquire one through a car accident or develop one through a serious illness. Everyone should be able to get what they need when they need it in order to lead as full a life as possible. This is clearly a socially responsible idea.'

Galbally referenced Shorten's speech at the same venue earlier in the year. 'When Bill Shorten addressed this forum in April, he said: "I make no apologies for seeing disability as an issue ... of basic civil rights." He went on to say, "I believe it is *the last frontier* of practical civil rights in this country." And he is right—this is a frontier that has been completely forgotten.'

Framed that way, the NDIS was the logical extension of what had preceded it in Australia's evolution—the fight for workers' rights to fair pay in the years after Federation, the rights to health care enabled by Medicare beginning in the 1970s, the fights for women's rights in the same decade. It could be the clinching achievement of progressive policy.

Galbally's argument was also based on economics.

'But what people don't understand is that the NDIS is also an economically responsible idea. The social insurance model, with its focus on the assessment of the lifelong needs of the individual, provides an incentive to reduce overall costs.

'Such a scheme will have an inbuilt incentive to maximise opportunities for participation and productivity. And because participation and productivity would be maximised, there would be savings not only in the disability service system but in health, income security and other programs.'

Galbally said the NDIS was also needed to help end discrimination. She told the story of a boy with Down syndrome who went to a cafe in a public park with some friends. Having become separated from them, he wandered around the park, lost. He came across some other children. Having younger siblings, he attempted to make friends with them. At that point, one of the fathers began shouting at him. Scared, he appealed to other adults. They shouted at him too. This, Galbally said, happens all the time—people with a disability, on average, have a negative social interaction within fifteen minutes of leaving their home. The silence in the room was palpable.

'We need this strategy to put an end to the daily discrimination experienced by people with a disability—in jobs, in life,' she continued.

'The issues raised in *Shut Out* will not be ignored. The voices in *Shut Out* will not go unheard. It is the right time.'

Rhonda Galbally persuaded a lot of people that day. And more persuasion was coming.

Again, there was one thing everyone agreed on by this time—securing sufficient funds was a necessary step for people with disability to participate fully in Australian life. And everyone could see that the massive amounts of money being allocated already weren't doing the job. It was hard to escape the conclusion that, *as things stood*, the amount needed was greater than any budget could supply, than any treasurer could reasonably commit to, given every other demand on the national budget.

This is the point where politics has to get creative—if the current solution does not fix the problem, a new solution is needed. And this problem wasn't going away anytime soon.

In the meantime, in the back rooms far away from the glare of exposure, the cogs had been turning in parallel with the *Shut Out* public hearings. A well-equipped, intellectually formidable team of economists and actuaries had been working away quietly and methodically to see just how a national disability insurance scheme could work. If the budget as it stood could not pay into disability what was needed, this team was looking for alternatives. It had been searching for a new solution. For a solution that would work long into the future. That team was the Disability Investment Group—DIG.

Left: Professor Kirsten Deane OAM, pictured with her daughter Sophie, was the campaign director for Every Australian Counts and is currently general manager of the Melbourne Disability Institute. (*Supplied*)

Right: John Walsh AM, considered one of the founding fathers of the scheme, was the original actuary. He was critical in taking the scheme from idea to reality. (*Supplied*)

Left: Australian Paralympic legend Kurt Fearnley was appointed chairman of the NDIA board in 2022, the first person with a disability to chair the board. He was a serving member of the NDIS's Independent Advisory Council during the trial phase from 2013 to 2015, and is a trusted disability advocate. (*Supplied*)

Right: Stella Young was one of Australia's fiercest advocates for people with disability. About the NDIS, Stella famously said: 'I don't think the question is whether or not Australia can afford to do this. It's how much longer can we afford not to.' Stella passed away in 2014. (*Fairfax Images*)

Bruce Bonyhady AM, pictured here with his sons, was one of the key architects of the NDIS and inaugural chair of the NDIA. A world authority on disability, he is currently co-chair of the Independent Review into the NDIS. (*Supplied*)

The Hon. Bill Shorten MP (centre), with Tim Walton (left), former president of the National Disability Services and chair of the Every Australian Counts steering committee, and Patrick Maher OAM (right), former National Disability Service chief financial officer, at the National Disability and Carer Congress in 2011: Make Every Australian Count.
(*Supplied by National Disability Services*)

Left: Dr Rhonda Galbally AC is one of Australia's foremost disability advocates and change agents. Dr Galbally, who has a lifelong disability, has been a CEO, chair and board member for more than 30 years. She was also the chair of the National People with Disabilities and Carer Council, which had the job of developing a national disability strategy. (*Fairfax Images*)

Right: Kevin Cocks AM is a lifelong Australian leader in human rights and disability. He served as the Queensland Anti-Discrimination Commissioner from 2011 to 2018. He brought considerable experience as a disability expert when the NDIS was being formed. (*Supplied*)

Left: Dougie Herd has worked for more than 30 years in disability advocacy, disability advice and service delivery in Scotland and Australia. He was in the senior executive leadership team of the NDIA at the birth of the scheme. Dougie is an NDIS participant. (*Supplied*)

Right: David Bowen was the inaugural chief executive of the NDIS and steered the scheme through its first five years. He was also a member of the independent panel that advised the Productivity Commission in its inquiry into a national disability care and support scheme. (*Every Australian Counts*)

A huge crown turned up in Penrith, NSW, for the Every Australian Counts rally in May 2012. More than 20,000 people attended these rallies around Australia to show support for the proposed NDIS. (*Every Australian Counts*)

Former Deputy Prime Minister Tim Fischer joins supporters of the Every Australian Counts campaign for the NDIS rally on the front lawns of Parliament House in Canberra in 2012. (*Fairfax Images*)

Thousands of people attended the Every Australian Counts rally at Federation Square in Melbourne to call for a National Disability Insurance Scheme in May 2012. (*Essential Media Communications*)

Former New South Wales Disability Minister John Della Bosca was the original Every Australian Counts campaign director. As well as being a seasoned campaigner, he worked closely with John Walsh on the concept of a no-fault scheme for people with disability in Australia, just as there was for people who had catastrophic injuries from road accidents. (*Supplied*)

Left: The Hon. Jenny Macklin AC was Minister for Families, Community Services and Indigenous Affairs from 2007 to 2010 and again in 2011 to 2013. Ms Macklin was the minister who oversaw the social policy reform and rollout of the NDIS. (*Getty Images*)

Right: The Hon. Julia Gillard AC was Australian Prime Minister from 2010 to 2013. She was integral in the NDIS being created and was the prime minister who introduced the NDIS Bill into Parliament on 29 November 2012. Almost six months later, in May 2013, Ms Gillard choked back tears as she introduced the legislation to fund the scheme. (*Getty Images*)

The Hon. Kevin Rudd AC was Prime Minister when the Productivity Commission was instructed to test the idea of the NDIS. (*Getty Images*)

The Hon. Mitch Fifield, a former Liberal Senator for Victoria, was the shadow minister for the disability, carers and voluntary sector from 2010 to 2013. Mr Fifield was the Assistant Minister for Social Services when the NDIS was rolling out across the nation from 2013. (*Fairfax Images*)

Former Prime Minister Julia Gillard and Victorian Premier Denis Napthine signing the heads of agreement between the Commonwealth and Victoria at Yooralla House in Reservoir, Melbourne in May 2013. (*Fairfax Images*)

Former Prime Minister Julia Gillard and Parliamentary Secretary for Disabilities and Children's Services Bill Shorten meet children with hearing difficulties and their parents at the Taralye centre for deaf children in Blackburn, Melbourne in 2010. (*Getty Images*)

The Hon. Bill Shorten MP at a rally in Melbourne to defend the NDIS in 2022. Shorten worked tirelessly to establish the NDIS as Parliamentary Secretary for Disabilities and Children's Services. As Opposition leader and shadow minister for the NDIS he fought to protect the scheme. In 2022 he was appointed to the position of Minister for the NDIS in the Albanese government. (*Essential Media Communications*)

'THE GENIE IS OUT OF THE BOTTLE'

———

JUST FOUR DAYS after the 2020 summit had recommended that a national disability insurance scheme be further investigated, the team that would carry out that investigation was announced. Bill Shorten had been putting it together long before the summit, but the summit gave him the impetus to announce it.

The focus for this team at the start, however, was not the scheme itself, but private sector investment. That was reflected in the group's name—the Disability Investment Group. That was where Shorten put the emphasis when announcing it.

'The Disability Investment Group will look closely at identifying and developing options for private investment in housing, education, employment, equipment and other support for people with disability,' he said. 'There is a real role the private sector can play here, and it is the Disability Investment Group's job to find out what barriers are stopping private investment, and what can be done to remove them.' This was in keeping with the thinking that Shorten had applied to the formation of the NPDCC, by going beyond the 'usual suspects', and bringing in businesspeople and union people who were not part of the established disability networks. It was also in keeping with his desire to go outside Canberra in his thinking and networking.

The chair of DIG was Ian Silk, the chief executive of Australian-Super, whose ultimate responsibility was the life savings of 2 million Australians. Shorten had sat on the board of AustralianSuper with Silk, but their relationship went back much further than that—to the 1980s, when Silk had been seconded from the bureaucracy to work in the office of state Labor minister Neil Pope, where they crossed paths. Shorten introduced Silk to Bruce Bonyhady.

Professor Allan Fels, well known as the former chair of the Australian Competition and Consumer Commission (ACCC), was also part of the DIG team, as was Bill Moss. He likewise had a significant public profile, formerly being head of banking and property at Macquarie Bank, and having done so much to turn a boutique bank into a global financial powerhouse. John Walsh, who we have already met, was a partner at PricewaterhouseCoopers who had made a lifelong study of lifelong care, was also on the team; as were Mary-Ann O'Loughlin, from the Allen Consulting Group, and Kathy Townsend, of Kathleen Townsend Executive Solutions.

'These members offer a wealth of experience and knowledge in philanthropic investment, including innovations to develop alternate funding assistance for people with disability and their families,' Shorten said at the time.

Looking back, he says his thinking when putting the team together was informed by his union background.

'One of the big problems in life is not that people are stupid or lazy, but a lack of power or a lack of money. So, follow the money. How do you get the money, and hence the political power. I'm a big believer in merit—but not all merit is equal. Some people have the merit but not the contacts—they didn't go to the right schools.

'So, find out who are the smartest people on a topic—that got me speaking to Bruce, and Allan Fels, and Bill Moss, and my old friend Ian Silk. I respect business success, but I like to deploy it in the interests of everyone, not just a shareholder or an owner. You go to smart business-people who have a wider world view than just making money—and that applies to all the people on DIG.

'The public service wasn't generating a discussion about alternative sources of income for disability. Not their thing. So, go outside Canberra. I'd always believed in the ethos, following Bill Kelty's thinking, that you're better off growing the pie—and then sharing it better. So, how to grow the pie in disability? Which then gives people a package to spend, which gives them agency. And that in turn creates a market, a market for services. If you've got empowered consumers with modest but reasonable packages of support, all of a sudden it will attract service to the world of disability, and generate some competition and some innovation. I believe in markets—and this would create a market for services. That was my hypothesis and I'd just tramp all around the country to sell it.'

Shorten had identified that the problem in the sector boiled down to the lack of funds. He also knew that simply going to the treasurer, or the prime minister, or the Expenditure Review Committee, and asking for more was not going to cut it. 'I had to battle with the fact that in the first budget, they mentioned the word "disability" once. Not Wayne's fault,' he adds, referring to treasurer Wayne Swan, 'that's just the way it was. Now, because I was the parly sec, I'm only looking at my patch and how that could get promoted. In the first budget, the word "disability" appears once; by the second budget, the word appeared twice. I did not consider this an entirely satisfactory state of affairs. So, how do we get the topic of disability from its powerless, moneyless state? The problem is carers and people with disabilities are so busy and tired just making ends meet. I thought we needed a common organising idea, and that's where the concept of an NDIS was percolated from.

'I realised there wasn't enough done in the employment space, in supported employment, in design, in transport, [about] day-to-day acts of discrimination, respite care. It became very clear to me almost immediately that everything's crisis driven and the only way you get attention is by being in crisis, which is the exact opposite of what we want. That's a dystopian world.

'But I'd been looking at how do I get more money into disability. Initially, I wondered if there were investment opportunities. So, I set up DIG, with Ian Silk to head it up. What I was trying to explain to Jenny [Macklin], and to everyone else, was that we needed money. You can't solve things, you can't make change, just using the existing funding. I was trying to work out how there could be a return on investment. I looked at the special disability trusts; they were good, but sort of only available for some people. I met John Walsh, who was excellent.'

Shorten set about meeting as many people who could help as he could, with the idea of bringing them together to see what they could come up with.

'I knew that we had to come up with a solution. I'd formed the view in 2008 that we needed a national disability scheme, but I didn't think the government agreed with that, so I thought, *How do I move my government along the spectrum?*'

It was obvious to Shorten that disability services were in a parlous state of affairs as they stood, and the warning signs that things would only get worse were clear.

'I just needed to get the claim going,' he says, like the lawyer he formerly was. 'Sometimes, I've learned in negotiations, you might not always know where you're going to end up, but you've got to get everyone on the same page to start the journey. And so, I did, I just organised it. By putting disability services on their agenda, the government had to accept that they had a problem, and therefore had to find a solution. I was happy to retrofit the logic.'

This was essentially the same strategy that Macklin referred to in terms of the *Shut Out* hearings—getting the problem out into an open space gave it visibility, and once it was visible, it would have to be fixed.

On the surface, that seems counterintuitive—it's the opposition who says we have a problem; the government who adopts the defensive position and says, *No, everything's fine.* Look more closely, though, and you will see that governments find problems all the time—it's the best way to justify change.

DIG was funded to the tune of $1.5 million, and supplied with staff and resources; also tapping PricewaterhouseCoopers' expertise to do some of the groundwork and costings. Senior public servant Helen Hambling headed up the secretariat, along with Lee Emerson, but both Bonyhady and Silk insist Hambling also played a huge role in developing ideas. Silk regarded her as an intrinsic part of the team—a de facto member of DIG.

The team members' economic, governmental and business backgrounds were not at all typical of those who usually made contributions to the sector. However, the DIG team was notable for some of its members having intimate knowledge of disability.

John Walsh was quadriplegic, because of an accident playing rugby league for the Newtown Bluebags thirds (before they were the Jets) in 1971, aged twenty. He crashed into a goal post, but continued playing, not realising he had damaged his spine until a week later, when he ran onto the field again and fell over.

Allan Fels' daughter, Isabella, had been diagnosed with schizophrenia in the 1990s, while he was head of the ACCC, which he detailed in an episode of *Australian Story.* He had first-hand experience of the bewildering nature of navigating the system to find his daughter help and, later, housing. Eventually, he and others formed their own housing group.

Bill Moss had a form of muscular dystrophy, which he has written about in his memoir, *Still Walking.*

Ian Silk recalls, 'I said to Bill, "I don't have any experience, direct or indirect, of disability. I feel like a bit of a fraud in this mob, mate." To which he said, "You can only see out of one eye, as I recall." Which is true. He continued: "That'll do for these purposes."

'In our initial conversation,' Ian Silk continues, 'Bill said to me, "I've got this portfolio. There is an extraordinary demand for service in the area. There are people receiving service but at inadequate levels, and people who have genuine needs who have no service. The common-wealth budget is not able to accommodate all of that demand. We'll need an alternative source of finance, some private finance. Can you lead a group to come up with some ideas about that?" So, that was our remit.'

~

Bruce Bonyhady remembers that at his first meeting with Shorten in January 2008, after the call in the aquarium, he knew who he wanted on the team. 'Bill chose the individuals. It was a very good group of people,' Bonyhady says. 'He went out and did the research. He put this group together.'

Ian Silk puts it thus: 'These are all very smart, well-connected, savvy, commercially astute people—but, frankly, we were spinning our wheels. We'd met on several occasions, but the ideas that we were generating were pissant sort of stuff. We were talking about depreciation on equip-ment for somebody who needed a wheelchair, for example; a tax subsidy for someone who needed to spend money to retool their house or what-ever. But it was sporadic, ad hoc, not systemic, not comprehensive. And not likely to have any material community-wide impact.' John Walsh agrees that the early ideas were not large enough to make a difference.

'Then our attention turned to the concept of the NDIS,' Silk con-tinues, 'and we agreed that, subject to Bill, who had convened our group, being happy, we would, in effect, junk all the work we had done and turn our mind to what an NDIS might look like. So, we spoke with Bill and he said, "Yeah. Go for it. See what you can do."' Things took off from there.'

Bonyhady recalls a similar development. 'Because John and I knew each other and thought we had the kernel of a very effective solution, we pushed very hard and the group agreed that we would undertake modelling of the costs of the NDIS. That's what we did. We commissioned PricewaterhouseCoopers and there were obviously some sensitivities around this, as John was then at PwC, but they produced the first costs of the NDIS.'

Walsh credits Rhonda Galbally for pushing the idea of expanding their thinking beyond accident compensation. 'Word started getting around that we were doing this. Rhonda Galbally started advocating that if you are going to do this, you really have to do the whole box and dice—extend it to disability.'

Galbally's recall is clear: 'I knew as soon as I heard about it that this idea would completely reform disability.'

DIG had conceptual questions that it had to consider from the outset. Would it go back to government with hundreds of recommendations, or take a holistic approach and instead recommend structural changes? If it went down the path of proposing an insurance scheme, what would be its boundaries? Who would it cover? Those injured, or those with innate disability? Which disabilities? How severe would they have to be? Would that include mental illness? Would it cover those who were already covered via states' motor accident schemes in Victoria, New South Wales and Tasmania? Would it be feasible to chop and change from one state to the next? Would it be a fully funded scheme or not? Would it address day-to-day living costs? How would it interact with the Disability Support Pension? And aged care? Would there be a cut-off point, probably related to age, where disability needs were not funded? What was the position of migrants and asylum seekers?

Some of the questions were settled very quickly, and work proceeded on the basis of those answers. Others would take time to resolve. Perhaps the first question was who this scheme would be for.

After due consideration, and after a lot of costings had been done, DIG concluded that a national insurance scheme was the best option, on many

fronts. 'We decided we would write a report which really only had one recommendation—that the government should do a further and full study of
the NDIS,' says Bonyhady. DIG did not settle on that decision until it had
sufficient costings from PricewaterhouseCoopers. 'We had done costings
that had indicated it was affordable,' Bonyhady confirms.

Ian Silk says: 'Bruce and John had done some work in this area, quite
a bit. John Walsh was at PwC and they were commissioned to do some
work on what an NDIS might look like, and they did quite detailed
work on the different cohorts of people who might be covered by the
scheme. The number of people, and what it might cost. We were conscious that financial sustainability would be an important dimension.
They did a power of work, brought it back periodically to our group, and
we would toss it around, challenge assumptions, suggest other areas to
look at. So, it was quite an interactive process.

'We spent some time talking about what the final recommendation
would be. It really wasn't for us to recommend to government to establish an NDIS. As comprehensive as PwC's work was, it was hardly a full
business case for the national government to sign off on. And so, we recommended that work be undertaken on the sustainability and viability
of a national disability insurance scheme.'

∾

Lee Emerson's position on the DIG secretariat gave her a vantage point
from which to view the big picture of how things were proceeding.

'There was a definite change within the group when they received the
PwC report,' she recalls. 'They decided, *We're just going to back this scheme
and run with it as a Big Thing.* And although they also landed on a few
other things, that was the transformational bit. People in the sector were
obviously attracted to it. The whole transformative nature then started,
and once it got pre-eminence, all of a sudden it became the agenda.'

Ian Silk concurs. 'I thought conceptually it was a great idea, but what was of concern essentially was how wide would the scope be, and therefore how big would the cost be. The work from PwC gave all of us a sense that a properly constructed NDIS could work well for those people most affected by disability, and their families and carers, and be able to be run on a financially sustainable basis. When we got the PwC report, that was the first time we thought, *This is a good idea and it might actually be able to be implemented on a sustainable basis.* That was the first time we could switch from a pure theoretical conception of what this might be like to a rather more data-driven assessment of what it might look like.'

Looking back, Silk recalls John Walsh as 'an amazing fellow. John was the person who gave DIG the intellectual grunt and substantiation that there was a business model here that could deliver it. That group was an extraordinary group. I was in awe of them as a collective. Allan Fels, a really serious thinker. Mary-Ann O'Loughlin was a social policy expert and knew the nuances of social policy like very few do. Bill Moss—my god, that man had drive. A real no-bullshit person. He wanted the meetings to drive on, not get lost in the fog of words, not get bogged down in meaningless discussion. He was terrific. Kathy Townsend was good, but had to leave us. Helen Hambling was as substantive a contributor as anybody. And Bruce—the indefatigable one who only saw obstacles as challenges to be overcome.'

ꙅ

There were multiple reasons to opt for a national insurance scheme—a key one was that the 'system' as it stood was not repairable. It was, in real estate terms, a knockdown. Trying to fix the system by patching it would only entrench the failures of the past long into the future, DIG quickly concluded.

That decision to opt for one big proposition, rather than many smaller ones, also had consequences for what happened immediately thereafter— if government were presented with one proposition, its answer would by definition be binary: yes or no. There may well have been some calculation that the answer if such a question were put to government would more likely be yes than no. Particularly in light of advocacy work being done, such as *Shut Out*, and the advocacy work to come.

The question of who to include was settled by thinking in terms of first principles, in terms of need—the purpose of the scheme was to address the needs of those who required assistance. Bonyhady explains: 'We took the view that it should cover all people with disabilities, and we included mental illness in the calculation. We saw this as equitable. For example, it didn't matter whether you had an intellectual disability, a physical disability, a sensory disability—it was your needs that would determine your eligibility, and this obviously also applied to psychosocial disabilities, which are often comorbidities with physical, intellectual, sensory disabilities.'

Jenny Macklin recalls that 'there was still debate about what it should be—should it be for all people with disability, should it be an accident compensation scheme. I didn't want it to go down the narrow path. That was the point at which I made what was perhaps the biggest decision of all—that it wouldn't be an accident compensation scheme, but should be for all people with profound or severe disability.'

DIG found that the goal should be meeting disability needs. Until this point, compensation, as we have seen, was terribly inequitable—if you had no insurance, if no insurance was available, if there was no one to sue, if no one was at fault, if the accident was inevitable ... then, bad luck, you were on your own. As we have also seen, that created the inequality that there could be two people with the exact same injury and one was compensated because the injury was sustained in a car accident, and one was not, because the injury was sustained in an assault. Or there could even be the situation where both people were in car accidents and sustained the same injuries but one was compensated because of being in a state with a compensation scheme, while the other was not.

Typically, compensation schemes are fully funded, in the sense that the system operates so that all the funds (insurance premiums) that come in one year will pay for all the costs (insurance payouts) in a particular year. Your coverage begins at the point you start paying your premiums. The situation here, though, was rather different: there were already hundreds of thousands of people living with disabilities. It was, quite simply, politically untenable for them to be excluded, not to mention unjust. These people would have to be accommodated. That was a major decision, perhaps inevitable, but one that had to be addressed because of its implications—typically, insurance schemes don't start with hundreds of thousands of people needing payouts before anyone has paid their premium. A fully funded scheme would need to have funds on hand for all the people already eligible, plus those who would be eligible in the coming years, and for their lifelong injuries. Paying this out of the interest on the pool of money would require an impossibly large amount. Which is why DIG opted for a pay-as-you-go scheme, in which there is no pool of money. 'I credit Allan Fels with coming up with the solution,' says Bonyhady.

The question of the interaction with the pension system was settled in a clear-cut fashion. The Disability Support Pension, which was increased substantially at this time, by seventy dollars a fortnight for singles and thirty dollars for couples, thanks largely to the efforts of Macklin, would remain, providing daily living costs for those unable to work. The insurance scheme would cover the costs of the disability.

DIG having settled many of these questions allowed contemplation of the big picture—what this scheme really was, how the nation would look upon it, how it should be presented to the nation.

Adam Smith's *The Wealth of Nations* is the theoretical work that undergirds capitalism, the publication of which coincided with the American Declaration of Independence. In the two-and-a-half centuries since he composed his work, Smith's meaning has been much contested, and much distorted. Over the past three to four decades, his name has often been invoked by the free-market fan clubs, the economic rationalists, the deregulators, the economic right, who all have him saying one thing: economies work best via the invisible hand (which is each person's self-interest), without the dead hand of government, and markets will always adjust so that the price is right for both buyer and seller, so everyone gets what they need. It is, of course, a cartoon characterisation of Smith's thinking; it also totally excludes his core moral philosophy, which is much to the contrary. Man, writes Smith, depends upon others far more than any animal does: 'In civilized society he stands at all times in need of the co-operation and assistance of great multitudes ... man has almost constant occasion for the help of his brethren.' Man's happiness and perfection, he wrote, 'is to feel much for others and little for ourselves, that to restrain our selfishness, to indulge our benevolent affections, constitutes the perfection of human nature'.

Smith's philosophy was on Bonyhady's mind. The argument that everyone is equal still holds sway in Australia—in demotic parlance, the 'fair go'. Presented this way, as a fair go, it would be very hard to argue against the NDIS, there to enable those with disabilities to have the life many aspire to—getting an education, getting a job, getting a place to live.

But the beauty of the concept of the NDIS was that it could be argued via the other side of the coin just as well—the NDIS is not simply for those people with disabilities, it is there for *you*. For your mother and your father. For your brother and sister. Your husband or wife. Your son or daughter. Because any one of you can have been born with a disability. And any one of you could become disabled at any moment. In fact, one person in Australia is diagnosed with a disability every half-hour. It could be you.

'I think, in terms of the way the arguments were structured for the NDIS, the fact that it was presented as an insurance scheme, which it is, made it relevant to all Australians, not just that group of people over there, even though they are deserving,' says Bonyhady. 'Adam Smith, the great economist, observed that people are both self-regarding and other-regarding. The self-interest is *This could happen to me; I could need it; a family member could need it*. And the other-regarding is that we've got this sense that this is something that we as a nation should do to ensure that people with disability get a fair go. That was one set of arguments that I think was very relevant.

'The other was that we framed it as an economic issue, so it was all about what it would add to GDP. Once you had it as an economic argument, then you had a way of running the gauntlet of treasury and finance departments. We therefore changed disability from what had been seen as a social issue or a disability rights issue into an economic issue.'

It's all about framing. Until now, help for those with disabilities had always been seen as welfare. Not any longer: the NDIS was not a welfare scheme. It was, as the name says, an insurance scheme. No one thinks of the various transport accident schemes as welfare. No one thinks of WorkCover schemes as welfare. They are not; they are insurance schemes. One of the great difficulties in large-scale governmental reform is first educating the public in order to persuade them; here, there was a perfect analogy, readily understood, and pretty much universally approved. Virtually no one today thinks of the NDIS as welfare. It's not. But, of course, it does improve the *wellbeing* of hundreds of thousands of people.

'Look at the best Australia-specific reforms—superannuation, the minimum wage, Medicare and now the NDIS,' says Shorten. 'These benefits are universal, not limited to a particular group of people, not means-tested, not rationed. Every Australian is entitled. They are not welfare but drivers of economic participation, in the case of the NDIS releasing those with disability from the tyranny of low expectations and also freeing their carers to work. As a middle-power nation of 26 million people occupying an entire continent, we simply can't afford to waste human potential.'

The idea that welfare is charity is always there, like background radiation, so that it never really goes away but nor does it completely rise to the surface. It is therefore never quite open to debate, which means it's an idea that can never be put to death. In that view, the age pension, unemployment benefits and the Disability Support Pension are charity, not entitlements—and charity has limits. These measures let you survive, and anything more is cream. But get the NDIS out of the welfare space, and suddenly that limitation is gone.

DIG's report, *The Way Forward*, also reframed this, noting that Australia's health system gives people an entitlement to health services, based on need, but there was no such entitlement to disability care and support services. The NDIS would remedy the issue that what services were available was not based on need, and that they were insecure and time-limited.

PricewaterhouseCoopers got costings and a draft report to DIG towards the end of 2008. Although the picture it painted was, in many ways, bleak, the conclusion it came to was thrilling: a national disability insurance scheme was affordable. And not just affordable: it could eventually pay for itself.

∽

PwC found that the $20 billion-plus being spent on disability annually—$8 billion on community care and support, $3 billion to carers and $11 billion to 700 000 people on the Disability Support

Pension—was a vast amount that failed to meet the relevant needs, which were expanding. Vast as it was, it was dwarfed by the replacement cost of the unpaid care provided by family members—estimated to be up to double that entire cost: $40 billion.

There were further hidden costs. The national health budget was running to $100 billion a year, and a huge percentage, expected to hit 80 per cent in coming years, was spent on people with a chronic or complex disease—many of these being people with disability.

And, of course, carers were ageing, and there lay a mathematical time bomb. A 10 per cent drop in the number of carers could mean the need for a 40 per cent increase in paid carers (mainly because unpaid carers do more than forty hours a week, and the number of informal carers was greater than the number of paid carers to start with).

Further demographic squeezes were applying even more pressure. Because the size of families had been consistently diminishing for so long, fewer carers would be available in the future. On top of that, the vast bulk of care has always been done by women, but women now work outside the home just as much as men do, reducing the future number of available carers even further.

The annual cost of the prison system was as much as $2.5 billion. More than half of the people in prison had either a mental illness or an acquired brain injury, which means that the cost of disability spilled over into spending on the prison system (and before that the judicial system that puts them in jail).

The incidence of disability increases with age, so an ageing population means a greater proportion of those with disability. PwC estimated the number of people with severe and profound disabilities would double within forty years, to 2.9 million—10.2 per cent of the population.

The conclusion: disability was costing more than we thought, and would cost much more in the future than we thought.

The report foresaw annual cost increases of 5 to 10 per cent a year just to remain steady—that is, to support a system that wasn't working.

∽

In October 2009 DIG lodged *The Way Forward* with the government.

'When the DIG was initially formed you [Bill Shorten] challenged us to think creatively about how to inject additional resources into the historically underfunded disability sector,' it began.

'In the course of lengthy discussions amongst ourselves, with people with disabilities, with family members and other carers who support people with disabilities, and with experts in the field, it became apparent that individual measures such as tax concessions to encourage additional private expenditure would, of themselves, be as useless as throwing a cup of water on a raging fire.

'Despite Governments spending around $20 billion annually on the disability welfare system (with billions more spent on other services in relation to people with disabilities) there remains a large, and rapidly growing, unmet need for care and support. This is despite an estimated army of 2.5 million family members and other carers providing unpaid care and support.

'The lack of proper planning and integrated service delivery is a national disgrace, and with increasing demand for, and increasing cost of, these services ... the situation for people with disabilities and their carers will undoubtedly worsen so long as the current arrangements remain in place.

'Accordingly DIG believes fundamental change is required.

'It is the strong view of DIG that structural reform is required in the framework governing disability policy in Australia. If this transformational shift occurs as suggested by DIG then the system would move from one based on short-term and often ad hoc resource allocation—with all of the inefficiencies and inequities involved—to a rational system where need, rather than happenstance, determines resource allocation. A whole new world of opportunities would be opened up for people with disabilities, and the families and other carers who support them.

'We believe that a National Disability Insurance Scheme (NDIS) is required to create the transformational shift to move care and support for people with disabilities out of the dark ages and into the 21st Century.'

It could not have been any clearer.

It could not have been any bolder.

It could not have been any more urgent.

Everything needs to change.

DIG was well aware of just how bold its plan was. As it stated: 'To lift Australia's record in assisting its citizens with disability to live the lives to which they aspire, the current disability system needs immediate and significant reform. This must be on the scale of the Medicare reforms or the introduction of compulsory superannuation.'

These were sobering words for any government to hear.

The pressure to act was building.

～

DIG recommended the NDIS as part of a three-pillar approach.

First, there would be the NDIS, to deliver lifelong care and support on an individualised basis; second, strong income support; and third, multiple measures to facilitate more private investment.

DIG focused mainly on the NDIS. The other two measures involved tax transfers, and would therefore have to cohere with the tax system, which, at the time, was undergoing the wholesale Henry Tax Review, in which everything was up for grabs. The change suggested by DIG was, as it noted, a transformational shift, totally rethinking how services were funded and delivered; reversing the focus, so that the person consuming the services was making decisions, not trying to fit in with the programs on offer. There was no underestimating the scope of the task: it would require a dedicated bureaucracy and attendant office space, it would have immense information technology demands, it would require a total remake of and increase in the service-delivery sector.

But perhaps DIG's most important finding—important because this element was possibly most likely to determine whether the idea ever became a reality—was this: 'DIG believes that ultimately an NDIS would be a net saving on government expenditure through a more effective service system, and better employment, health and social outcomes for people with disability.'

The social insurance model it proposed would work this way: assess the mathematical risk of disability across the population, calculate the cost of servicing that disability across a lifespan and estimate the premium from taxpayers to meet those needs.

It suggested two funding methods: either from government general revenue, or a levy, like Medicare.

How could such a vast scheme save money?

Insurance principles would underpin it—and a golden rule of insurance is to invest early to reduce long-term costs. To invest in rehabilitation, in support. As we have seen, the current system did the opposite: those in crisis attracted the most funds, meaning that problems got out of hand before they were dealt with. The opposite applies under a well-run insurance scheme. In an insurance scheme, premiums are invested to maximise long-term returns, and claims are actively managed—that is, monitored with feedback from recipients, which improves both efficiency and effectiveness.

Three other main areas were identified as being in need of development—areas that would bring great financial dividends, as well as social ones.

Employment opportunities needed to be improved. DIG noted that, according to the OECD, Australia came thirteenth out of nineteen countries in the employment rate for those with disability. Worse, this rate was falling, while in other countries it was climbing. OECD figures also placed Australia last out of twenty-seven countries in the number of people with disability living on or below the poverty line. Australia did worst when it came to providing benefits for anyone with a disability and working—due to the fact that the system had built-in disincentives against working. Only 11 per cent of those receiving disability benefits were doing any paid work. The gross personal income of someone with a disability was half that of someone without.

DIG's research had found great resistance by the private sector to finding workers via the government's Disability Employment Services; DIG recommended instead directing people into the mainstream jobs market. It was clear that more, many more, people with disabilities could work—the calculation was that finding jobs for 140 000 people over ten years would bring a saving of $1.6 billion in the Disability Support Pension. At the time, 700 000 people were on it, with about 70 000 new entrants a year, nearly all of whom never got off it, except to move across to the age pension. The figure of 140 000 people finding jobs was a reasonable assumption, matched against the recovery rates of seriously injured people—many of whom had suffered catastrophic injuries—who moved from WorkCover back into work.

Getting better job outcomes for people with disability would also return revenue to government, via the tax paid on wages. This would run into the tens and eventually hundreds of millions of dollars.

DIG recognised that people with disability face extra costs when taking up work, and suggested a disability support tax rebate to encourage them to work—which it acknowledged would be subject to the Henry Tax Review. It urged the removal of taxes on essential goods and services required by people with disability, their families and carers;

as well as changing duty on imported vehicles, footwear, clothing and goods used extensively by people with disability. That might cost the government in the short term, but would provide a greater return by helping get people into the workforce.

DIG discovered a hidden trap it wanted removed: people accessing Australian Disability Enterprises for what is informally known as work in sheltered workshops were barred from accessing the Disability Employment Service, which could get them into so-called open employment. Changing this would also increase work participation.

Getting more people with disability into work would bring down the cost of carer payments—the figures showed clearly that carers were more likely than non-carers to be unemployed or underemployed. They would be freed up to work, once again providing a return to government via their taxes.

These are the financial benefits. As well, we all know being in work goes a long way towards ending social isolation and exclusion, and their accompanying poor health outcomes, both mental and physical.

Added together, the savings and benefits of the NDIS meant the scheme would pay for itself in the long run—and the 'long run' was estimated as being fifteen years.

The exponential curve of the growth of unmet needs was becoming steeper as carers either died, were themselves admitted into care, or simply gave up because they could not cope any longer. Plotting those increases against the projected costs of the NDIS, things would be less costly—and infinitely better—within one generation. The savings would then multiply down the generations. That was the calculation even when including the health-care costs of treating people with conditions such as cancer, who might be better off out of disability care and in the health system.

About half the people in aged care in 2008 had incurred a disability before the age of sixty-five. In years to come, those people would be taken care of via the NDIS, lifting the burden on the aged care system, which itself is enormous—the fastest-growing budget expenditure item, expected to double to 2 per cent of GDP around the middle of the century. Although DIG's proposed cut-off age to make an NDIS claim was sixty-five, people already covered would be allowed to continue on it past that age, thus relieving the aged care system. These savings would be stupendous—estimated by DIG to be up to half the cost of the aged care system—and would only increase over time.

Although not quite in the same stratospheric financial realms, the assessed savings in relation to reducing homelessness and the burden on the criminal justice system, including prisons, were also significant. DIG compared the 30 000 people in supported accommodation with the 25 000 people in prison. It costed a year in prison at between $70 000 and $100 000 per person—a total cost of between $2 billion and $2.5 billion. It cost less to have someone in care.

DIG pointed to a New South Wales housing and accommodation scheme for 110 people with mental illness and psychiatric disability, which reduced their time spent in hospital by 80 per cent, with a similar reduction in prison time. As, again, more than half of the prison population suffers mental illness or acquired brain injuries, that would, applied nationally, be a saving well in excess of $1 billion a year. (It was even potentially approaching $2 billion, although DIG preferred to model conservatively.) There would be further cost savings in reducing court time, and the various costs of crime—property damage, insurance claims, WorkCover claims and, yes, those who incurred a disability as a result of crime. And these, of course, are just the financial benefits; the social benefits are arguably greater.

DIG also had big ideas in relation to housing, noting that the United Nations Convention on the Rights of Persons with Disabilities recognises the right to an adequate standard of housing. Enormous financial benefits could be had in this space, for relatively low cost. Even though housing took up a disproportionate amount of the disability budget, it still represented the area of greatest unmet need. People with disability constituted 40 per cent of those living in public housing (a figure that had doubled in five years). That spending was further supplemented by the rental assistance helping those in the private rental market. Supported accommodation was funded by a variety of sources: the National Disability Agreement (formerly the CSTDA), disability organisations, philanthropy, fundraising and parents. Service providers often delivered part- or fully funded accommodation. DIG recommended that nexus be broken, to avoid client capture, whereby someone accepts second best because there is no alternative, and also as being in keeping overall with the client-first model.

The problem was that the disability housing sector was not sufficiently profitable to attract commercial investment. The government had recently introduced the National Rental Affordability Scheme, which encouraged and, in effect, subsidised the provision of low-income housing. DIG was of the opinion that the incentives were not great enough to facilitate disability-friendly housing, and that the scheme should be amended accordingly.

It urged the government to explore further ways to encourage family and private investment in housing. An area of major concern was building regulations, which, DIG said, needed urgent action. It argued that all new housing should be made to accommodate disability—27 per cent of the population was projected to have a disability by 2051. Many people have to move out of their homes and into care simply because their home is unlivable—perhaps only because of an inaccessible bathroom. Or doorways that are too narrow. Or a kitchen that is too small to accommodate a wheelchair. The extraordinary cost of aged care to the federal budget could be vastly reduced by getting housing right in the first place. DIG recommended a mandatory accessible path from a parking area to the home's entry; a ground-floor bathroom with reinforced walls to allow for a hobless shower (the hob being the little barrier at ground level at the shower's entry that keeps the water in); a minimum doorway width of 850 millimetres; corridor entry width of 1000 millimetres; and enough space in the kitchen to turn a wheelchair. If implemented, such simple, low-cost measures could allow hundreds of thousands of people to age in their homes, saving potentially billions of dollars in the long run, and keeping these people independent and happy.

After the NDIS and regulatory changes, the third pillar was to establish a centre of excellence for disability research, with an extended role in data collection; the centre would be run by the NDIS. Although PwC did an extraordinary job mustering the data to cost the scheme, it identified many holes in the disability database, which was uncoordinated, diffuse and poorly shared. Research had long been neglected, receiving just $400 000 a year under the CSTDA, then jumping to $2 million a year for the next five years. DIG suggested $30 million a year. The more data an insurance scheme has, the more cost-effectively it can run, by better calculating and accounting for risk in advance.

Aside from being necessary for good policy, research also offered the potential to be commercialised and exported, through the development of links to the corporate sector. This meant that besides the savings the research would generate, it could even turn a profit.

～

On 23 November 2009 Prime Minister Rudd, Jenny Macklin and Bill Shorten attended the National Disability Awards night at Parliament House. Two years earlier, in the first flush of electoral success, Macklin and Shorten had been in attendance and promised something big: the ministerial council that had proved so influential.

Everyone at the awards in 2009 had been keeping abreast of developments: the hearings that had resulted in the groundbreaking *Shut Out*, which put faces to the stories of those with disability; followed hot on its heels by DIG's detailed economic analysis, which had recommended everything be changed through the introduction of a national disability insurance scheme.

Rudd had something even bigger to announce tonight: the government would commission a thorough feasibility study of the NDIS.

'The Productivity Commission inquiry will examine the feasibility, costs and benefits of replacing the current system of disability services with a new approach which provides long-term essential care and support for people with severe or profound disabilities, however acquired,' he said.

'The inquiry will examine a range of options for long-term care and support, including consideration of whether a no-fault social insurance approach to disability is appropriate in Australia. It will also examine if a scheme would fit with Australia's health, aged care, income support and injury insurance systems.

'These are complex issues that require rigorous analysis, design and costing. The Productivity Commission will consult widely and will be assisted by an associate commissioner with specialist disability expertise. An independent panel of experts will also be established to advise the Productivity Commission and government during the inquiry. The Australian Government will appoint the associate commissioner and the independent panel of experts shortly.

'The Productivity Commission will report to government in July 2011.'

Everyone in the room was thrilled. Tears, once again, were shed. What had seemed a pipedream less than two years before had just taken one giant, necessary step towards becoming a reality.

Shorten had sat on the DIG report throughout 2009, awaiting the right moment. During the year, its contents had been massaged by him and Macklin in conjunction with the DIG team. Its release was orchestrated in concert with *Shut Out*. This was a one-two punch: the stories that revealed the great human needs in the sector, plus the economic case arguing how these needs could be met.

'Timing isn't the main thing—it's *every*thing,' Shorten says.

Shorten had been timing his run, like a good jockey. The NDIS was such a big idea that it was always going to take time. And he was starting at a handicap, being one step below a minister and a new boy. 'I didn't have any muscle in Canberra on day one. They all had their own ideas. And parliament is like a horrendous, toxic boarding school—the new boy has to wait his turn. But I thought their ideas would run out of petrol. And I knew that come the election for a second term, the government would need a new big idea. They would have to go to the big-idea shop and get one wrapped up off the top shelf. Well, here it was.'

Thus armed, he, via Macklin as his senior minister, had gone to cabinet with a proposal, arguing for the Productivity Commission (PC) to examine further the case for an NDIS. 'I agitated and agitated, I put together a submission, and presented it to cabinet. And I remember one senior cabinet minister saying, "Don't you go raising expectations here." I mean, c'mon—we're the Labor Party, we're in the hope business.

'Once we had the idea that the NDIS could be subject to the PC, we're off to the races,' he says. On leaving the cabinet meeting, he rang Bruce Bonyhady to tell him: 'The genie's out of the bottle.'

～

The awards night was also notable for another event. One that appeared out of the blue, but as if on cue.

One of the attendees was Kurt Fearnley. He was well known to the public for three appearances at the Paralympic Games, with two more to come in the years ahead. By the time he retired from competition, he had thirteen Paralympic medals to his name, three of them gold, in middle- and long-distance wheelchair races. That level of achievement was a far cry from what doctors had predicted for him at his birth in Cowra, New South Wales, in 1981—imminent death, thanks to a congenital disorder that prevented the development of his spine.

In November 2009 he decided to do the Kokoda Track: the 96-kilometre mountainous path in Papua New Guinea, where Allied soldiers, mainly Australian, fought off the invading Japanese during World War II. It is treacherous, high-altitude stuff, the days hot and humid, the nights severely cold. If you are champion runner John Landy, you can cover the distance in four days. Mere mortals commonly take twelve. That year, 2009, four people had died attempting the Kokoda Track before Fearnley set out.

He, however, would be doing something no one had done before: he would crawl the distance. A wheelchair simply could not navigate the course. That inconvenience would not stop Fearnley, who always liked to take himself out of his comfort zone. There would be nothing comfortable about crawling through the mud of the Kokoda Track, besieged by mosquitoes, sweaty and dirty, his limbs protected by specially made guards. Yet he recognised that the diggers had done it harder than he would—they were in danger of being killed. Many were. 'They did it so much harder than we can even imagine,' he said. He had trained for the previous twelve months by climbing stairs, but, even so, the rigours of the track were more difficult than he anticipated; so tough that he considered quitting along the way. 'Mate, I just was hurting. It was the toughest thing I've ever done,' he said when he reached the end point.

Fearnley was doing all this for charity: in particular, Movember, which raises awareness of men's mental health; encouraging them to speak up and to each other about their feelings. Having grown up in Carcoar, New South Wales, a town of 200 people, Fearnley was well aware of the reticence of Australian men to express their pain, acknowledge their vulnerability and ask for help.

Imagine his indignation when he arrived at Brisbane Airport on the way home from Papua New Guinea to be told that he would have to check in his wheelchair as luggage for the connecting flight to Newcastle and, in the meantime, use an alternative wheelchair, one he could not propel himself, pushed by an attendant. 'I said there is not a chance that I am going to sit there and be pushed through an airport,' he recounted at the awards night. 'An able-bodied equivalent, a normal person's equivalent, would be having your legs tied together, your pants pulled down and be carried or pushed through an airport.'

When talking to the media the next day, Shorten said, 'Kurt crawled the Kokoda Track, a feat which all Australians think is remarkable, but he didn't expect to crawl across the tarmac when he gets into Australia.'

No one at the awards night needed reminding of the indignity often inflicted upon those with disability, but the story of Kurt Fearnley crawling through Brisbane airport after crawling the Kokoda Track opened the eyes of many Australians.

THE POLITICS OF HOPE

———

RHONDA GALBALLY CALLED a meeting in her North Melbourne office in early 2009. Bill Shorten had urged her to unite and mobilise, and that was what she was doing.

Present was Lesley Hall, who had been fighting the fight since that headline-gathering intervention at the beauty contest in St Kilda Town Hall in the 1970s. She represented those with disability, as CEO of the Australian Federation of Disability Organisations. Representing the carers were Pam Webster and Joan Hughes, the chair and CEO of Carers Australia.

The meeting was a bringing together of the tribes. The ministerial council that Galbally headed was the first step in the process; the new groups she was forming would be its culmination, and this meeting was its beginning. From here on, disability groups and the carers' group would work together, and be welded together, in the pursuit of one common objective: the NDIS. They would do so via a campaign called Every Australian Counts.

'There was a terrible standoff between people with disabilities and carers previously,' Galbally recalls. 'The discourse from carers so often was about the "burden" on them of their loved ones—people with disabilities. And there's still a sense of sadness when that discourse is raised. But in that meeting, the reality from the carer perspective was really understood by those of us with disabilities. It was really a meeting about empathy and understanding different experiences of disability. At the meeting, it became bearable for the carer lobby to understand the pain that characterising disability as a burden caused people with disabilities. At the same time, it became bearable for people with disability to understand the pain (and burden) carers felt. It was a moving coming together, one of those moments I'll never forget. It was powerful for me personally, thinking about my mother and her experience as different to mine. It wouldn't have happened if those people hadn't been in the room—Lesley Hall and Joan Hughes.'

After this meeting, Ken Baker, the head of National Disability Services, the peak body of the service providers, would be invited to join them. The three divisions would come together to form the National Disability and Carer Alliance.

The split between these different divisions might look, on the surface, from a distance, to be a matter of goals, of perspectives. But it goes much, much deeper than that—to the heart, to how a person feels about themselves and in relation to their loved ones. It touches the essence of their humanity. To hear parents talking about the 'burden' of their child turns that child into a burden, not a loved family member.

Ara Cresswell was soon to succeed Joan Hughes as CEO of Carers Australia. Not long after her appointment, she was confronted, and shocked, by the depth of the division.

'When I went to Carers Australia, one of my friends who has a disability said to me, "How could you join the enemy?" It really struck me. I thought, *I don't know any family with a member who has a disability who could be seen as the enemy*. I can understand that some people with disability have been treated appallingly [by their family], left on their own in soiled clothes, but in all the time I spent working with families, I've not seen those families. I've only seen the families who will do anything for their family member. We love our family member with a disability and want to be sure they have the best possible life.'

What had to be done was to heal this wound, end this split.

Galbally had already healed her deepest split—with her mother, which she writes about in her book *Just Passions*. That split had been 'embodied in the Carer movement ... It was as though an identity as a Carer was developed without disability being on the agenda at all ... It reminded me very much of not being able to hear my mother's pain about me being disabled, so her pain took on a life of its own—a dull dissatisfaction at the unfairness of life.' Galbally would take on the care of her ageing mother, but not call herself her carer—simply her daughter.

Rhonda Galbally was one year old when the polio virus swept across Australia in the 1950s. An ambulance took her to hospital. Her mother and father were not allowed to go with her—she was deemed infectious. That night, her father went to the local phone box to call the hospital to check that his baby daughter was still alive. When he got the good news, he hung up, turned around, and there was Mrs Muir, a neighbour. He thought, *How wonderful, coming out to comfort me like this.* Mrs Muir held up her bottle of disinfectant. 'I've come to wipe out the box—especially the receiver. We don't want anyone to catch polio,' she said. Welcome to the world of disability.

'I think disability is an even more confronting reality than race,' says Galbally. 'There is such a push for them to be better off put away—out of sight, with their own kind, so you don't have to look at them, or be with them, to not be contaminated. It's a deep apartheid. The most egregious attitude is that the disability is all there is. There's a giving-up on people with disabilities.'

Children such as Rhonda Galbally were often put in institutions. Often for life. They tended to die young, for many reasons, inadequate health care being one. Galbally's parents weren't having that. First, however, there were two years in hospital. Parental visits were limited to an hour a fortnight—the hospital wanted compliant babies, not ones crying when their parents left. But return home Galbally did, to live a life not limited by disability. So, here she was now, setting out on a new adventure as head of the newly formed National Disability and Carer Alliance—which had work to do.

Whereas the ministerial council Galbally had headed had been as large as possible, with twenty-eight members, the membership of the Alliance was kept deliberately small, for a strategic reason: to maintain unity and speak with one voice.

Bill Shorten had urged the idea of this alliance on Galbally. 'My job was to be a coach, an enabler, a facilitator,' says Shorten, 'but I did have to teach them to focus on one thing. Don't ask the politicians first, ask everyone else, so then it becomes too hard to say no. I was very keen on the idea of grassroots action. So, I encouraged the formation of Every Australian Counts. I just said to all the disability peak bodies and leaders, "We need to bypass the politicians, and start getting the people into it and get them agreeing on the common demand."'

Bruce Bonyhady, who was an associate member of the Alliance, had many conversations early on with Galbally about its shape and goals. He knew it was important to win the support of *all* political parties—and the best way to do that was to win the support of the public. 'That was strategic—we went into the campaign thinking that, but it was also extraordinary execution.'

They were also thinking about unity, and how best to achieve and preserve it. 'We decided that the Alliance would be unwieldy if we allowed every organisation to join, and we had many organisations that were keen to join us as the momentum grew. We took the view that a consensus approach was essential.' So, it was kept small.

The Alliance set itself one goal: get the NDIS.

To do so, it agreed to put aside all differences in that quest. 'That seems the obvious thing to do,' says Ken Baker, but he says it was easier said than done. 'It was quite a job—there were always some members opposed, someone saying, *What are we doing getting into bed with that mob for?* We got to the point of maturity, where we set aside the twenty per cent of things we disagreed on, or we agreed to debate them around the table rather than in public, and got to work on the eighty per cent of things we did agree on. And in particular, this chronic, unmet need for support for services, which we all agreed was huge and urgent and important, and we would work together on that. We achieved historic unity across the sector. I think we produced a very powerful united voice to the community and to government, which was what the politicians, what Jenny Macklin, told us we must do.'

The Alliance agreed that the way to get the NDIS was to persuade Australians—and, in turn, their parliamentary representatives—that the NDIS was a good thing, a necessary thing.

It was soon paying dividends: the ACTU, the Australian Medical Association and the Pharmacy Guild quickly signed up to support the scheme.

う

Ara Cresswell remembers 'this feeling of great excitement. I was at one of the first rallies in Sydney with Ken Baker, from National Disability Services, a conservative man, so often the butt of people's fury over services, and a conservative dresser. We were all wearing the red T-shirts with *Every Australian Counts* on them. Ken came in his standard shirt, trousers and tie, and I said, "Ken, put this on." I had a bright red fake leather cap and a bright red scarf, and put them on Ken, and we took photos, and everybody's going "Kennnnnnn!"—we were all so excited about what was happening, that together we could do this. To see Ken trotting around in this very strange outfit was quite exciting, to see him caught up in the excitement with the rest of us, making this thing happen. This was going to change the lives of people with disability.'

The 'this' that Cresswell is referring to is the Every Australian Counts campaign—the major public-facing work that the Alliance did, persuading Australia of the absolute necessity of the NDIS.

A year in the making, the campaign kicked off on Australia Day 2011, and ran for years thereafter. The website is still live, closely monitoring all the scheme's continuing developments.

The Australia Day launch was no coincidence—one of the appeals the campaign made was to patriotism. The paucity of resources devoted to disability in government budgets compared unfavourably with those of other countries. Australia could do better, the campaign urged. And it appealed, above all, to the deepest, most commonly held, and perhaps defining, Australian value—a fair go. People with disability deserved a fair go, just like everyone else.

By a stroke of luck, the campaign recruited John Della Bosca, the former New South Wales minister for disability, as its director. 'I came out with the idea that we should launch the campaign on Australia Day, and we should focus on fairness and the Australian idea of a fair go, and that we should call the campaign Every Australian Counts. The reason for that was the idea that every Australian counts, which was a kind of deliberate double entendre; [it] was obvious that they all count, and that they all vote.

'And not everybody was all that sympathetic to this. When I first went through this as our campaign positioning, quite a few people said, "We always talk about compassion, we talk about empathy, we don't talk about patriotism," and I said, "How far has that got us?" We needed to motivate people more strongly.'

Speaking like a man from the New South Wales Labor Right, Della Bosca says, 'I've always thought that the idea of the Australian characteristic of a fair go was basically bullshit. I don't know that it's truly part of a national character or even that a national character exists, but I almost changed my own mind because [of what] seemed to happen during the campaign.'

His appointment was not without debate—some would have preferred to hire a person with a disability. The campaign was also meant to be apolitical, in the sense of appealing to all MPs, no matter what their party, without boosting any party at the cost of any other; a former Labor MP could be seen as partisan, making him a risky appointment. But Della Bosca had the skills, the drive, the nous and the networks. He knew how to campaign. As well as deciding on a patriotic tinge to the campaign, he was the one who emphasised that it had to be relentlessly positive. He knew all too well that MPs are weighed down by requests day in, day out, for this, that and the other thing. The campaign would ask for but one thing, which, in a sense, cost nothing: it would ask people, and their MPs, to say yes to this idea. Della Bosca's Labor presence was balanced by the appointment of Tim Fischer, former National Party leader and deputy prime minister, as the first patron of Every Australian Counts. 'My family has been touched by disability,' he said at the time, referring to his son Harrison, who is autistic, 'and I know first-hand our disability system is broken. In regional Australia it is even worse. Families have limited access to respite, can wait years for equipment and often have to move long distances to find a place for their children to live.'

Ara Cresswell concurs on the goals of the campaign. 'What we saw was a whole lot of families take that opportunity to get out and spread the message, eventually to their local MPs, really advocating. People could write letters as part of the campaign. We hit pretty much every politician—that was our aim, so that when this came up for a vote we had support across all parties.

'We were really clear we had to make this about the person with disability—not about politics, because politics would have destroyed it.'

The goal was to convince the nation. That requires money, which the Alliance did not have. There would be no national advertising, which is expensive, and there would be no Canberra lobbying; those firms don't come cheap. No, this would be a grassroots campaign mounted by the very people who needed the NDIS—people with disability and their carers. All the organisations that could contributed what money they had; plus, there was a little government advocacy money, with National Disability Services providing the bulk, helped along by its 1100 member organisations. A decision that was taken out of necessity turned into a strength—it was the faces and the stories of people with disability that were persuasive in the end.

Rob White, then at the Spastic Centre and now CEO of successor body Cerebral Palsy Australia, was in charge of fundraising. He had known Bruce Bonyhady for some years. 'His kids were clients of ours, here in New South Wales. He made a suggested improvement, and I asked my staff, "Who is this guy?", and they said "Oh he's amazing, a high-powered banker, who brings his kids in, he gets in the hydro pool with them." We hit it off pretty well. So years later I'm in Melbourne, we catch up for a coffee, and he started to talk to me about this idea he's had, for a national insurance scheme.'

White saw Bill Shorten on *Q&A* in 2008 and was so impressed with the answer he gave to the mother of a child with autism that he sent him an email, noting that he was at last getting disability on the agenda, which resulted in a meeting. 'He was staying at Palm Beach at [Labor gadfly] Bob Ellis's place, and asked would I like a coffee, so we got together,' White recalls.

'At the time we couldn't meet the needs that were walking through the doors. The system was broken. You might get $10 million if you could sue for medical negligence—otherwise you might get nothing. Bill knew that. Anyway I ended up leading the campaign to get up a fighting fund to get the NDIS. I started to go to other disability organisations, and we held lunches and got them to come in and pledge, $50,000 a year for the larger organisations for three years. We set up a website which turned into the Every Australian Counts campaign. Most of the service providers came to the party—they could see this as the light on the hill, and that it was worth fighting for.'

Kirsten Deane was there from the start, as deputy to Della Bosca. 'It was my job both to run the Alliance and to put together a bigger group of people who could run a campaign. What would a campaign look like? What would it take to pull it off? What resources would we need? What people would we need? How would it work?'

In the middle of 2010, the big mining companies mounted a campaign against the so-called Super Profits Tax, the one big idea Kevin Rudd had decided to implement out of the Henry Tax Review, which was the one big idea out of the 2020 summit he had backed immediately. The miners had no shortage of funds—they mounted an expensive nationwide multimedia ad campaign and a sophisticated lobbying exercise just at the wrong time for Rudd. He was swiftly removed as prime minister, and his successor, Julia Gillard, dumped that tax.

'But we weren't the mining industry,' Deane says. 'We didn't have that money. Our campaign wasn't about paying fancy consultants to walk the halls of parliament. It wasn't about buying advertising. A campaign like this takes resources, and we hardly had any.

'What we did have was this amazing, passionate community who wanted to see change. They were resource-poor, time-poor, they lived in poverty, they were already hanging on by the skin of their teeth. And here we were, going, "Oh, by the way, could you go out and do another thing?" You're asking people who are already facing incredible challenges day to day, "Oh, by the way, could you become a campaigner?"

'And they did. It was genuinely a grassroots campaign, which was the best way for our people to explain what their life was like—and what it could be like if they had proper support. Through the NDIS.'

To persuade people that the NDIS was the answer, they first had to know what the problem was. The problem, of course, was the barriers that prevented people with disability leading a full life.

'So, our job was to enable people to tell their story,' says Deane. 'Give them the training. Give them a platform.'

There were many platforms. One of them was the Every Australian Counts website, which had a counter front and centre showing the number of people signing up in support. It said, 'Count me in'. The number on the counter—part of Della Bosca's double entendre—grew every day, creating a sense of momentum that was visible to the people campaigning.

When the website launched, it revolved around five stories—those of Peter, James, Claire, Robert and Mary, and Billie. 'I do like to really emphasise that people told their stories in their own words,' Deane says. 'We weren't telling them what to say, they told them. It was the way they told their stories that made them so powerful.' They avoided the binary clichés into which media stories typically fell: stories of great courage, stories of great hardship.

No one who saw the good-natured Peter, from Mandurah, Western Australia, could forget him. He told how, as a boy, he was swimming with mates under the old Mandurah bridge when one of them jumped and landed on him, breaking three neck vertebrae and resulting in instant paralysis. Nine months in hospital followed. Peter, twenty-five years old when telling his story, worked at the Mandurah Council. If he stayed home and did nothing, he'd get about forty hours from support workers. Because he worked, he got only ten, which made his work more difficult. What Peter wanted was support to enable him to work more productively. 'Things have to be going bad before you get help,' Peter said—again, the crisis-driven system had adapted to its crisis-driven nature to the point that it helped *only* when things got bad.

He said he had thought his life was over when he was paralysed because that's all you ever hear. 'So why not start promoting the things you can do?' Peter asked. He said the NDIS would help because supports would be available instead of him having to battle for every single thing that could help him.

Then there was the clearly intelligent James, twenty, who had spastic quadriplegia cerebral palsy and was studying commerce at university while working as a marriage celebrant. With parents in their sixties, James was worried about what would happen when they could no longer provide the 24-hour care he needed. 'The NDIS would give me the opportunity to plan for the future and not worry about these transitions all the time,' he said. Transitions are the vulnerable point—when everything has to be applied for all over again, and the misery lottery comes back into play. Throughout school, a carer had given James support, but when he transitioned to TAFE, he had to write letters to all manner of authorities—heads of departments, the premier—pleading to get the same support. Then it was the same process all over again when he went to uni—where support was denied, until he wrote to the prime minister and Bill Shorten. While awaiting answers, his mother attended night classes with him after she finished her day job. 'That was very demanding,' James said. 'I felt very excluded. All of that was due to red tape.' Lifelong support on the NDIS would remove the stress and anxiety of those transitions, he explained.

Claire—a mother, a counsellor for the town of Victoria Park, Western Australia, author and life coach—had muscular dystrophy and used a wheelchair. She could not access her front door, and could not pay for alterations, or get support to do that. So, she used a side gate, which she could not padlock. Her house was broken into while she was at home. 'Why don't I count?' she asked. The NDIS would help make her home fit for purpose. And secure and safe.

Mary told the story of her son Robert, twenty-eight, born three months premature, who then had a brain haemorrhage at birth. Blind and paralysed, Robert, too, is quite intelligent. Mary's concern was for her son's dignity—as an adult, he no longer wished to be washed by her. 'We're in a charity welfare system. In a first-world country like Australia, people with disability should not be asking for charity. They should be given basic needs without having to beg for them,' she said calmly. The NDIS would put an end to begging. 'Robert would be able to choose what's best for him, and that's very important.'

Billie told the story of her son, Kai. They had attended countless campaign events and met Prime Minister Gillard at one. Kai died in 2018, and, out of respect, their story is no longer available on the website.

All of these people told their stories with great dignity and no self-pity. And more videos were to follow.

'The fact that people with disability were telling their stories in the way they wanted to tell them was, I think, what was really powerful,' Deane says. 'People with disability had control. We had to work pretty hard with the media, not to, you know, fall back into those old tropes.

'We were actively trying to promote positive attitudes towards people with disability. If we had done anything that reinforced any negative attitudes towards disability, while we may have won the NDIS, we would have won the battle but lost the war.'

Deane likes to give two examples of campaigners. One was a woman named Lyn who used to take a card table to her local supermarket every day, sit outside, and 'hassle people to sign the petition of the NDIS'. Lots of Geelong shoppers remember Lyn. 'The success of the campaign was completely down to the Lyns of this world,' says Deane.

The other example is Deane's mum—'not a political person at all, never been to a rally, not her jam. She held a DisabiliTEA with her book club and got them to sign up.'

DisabiliTEAs involved people inviting others to their homes, telling them about disability and getting them to sign the petition. There were thousands of DisabiliTEAs all across the country, many in workplaces. Ken Baker saw to it that disability service providers also put on

DisabiliTEAs, inviting as many people as they could, including local MPs, which he thinks was vital. 'We talked about this in the context of where you live, not just as some abstract idea or some national issue. It was a local issue.'

Rob White and Bonyhady, meanwhile, were hosting lunches for large corporations, explaining the NDIS concept to them, and winning their publicly pledged support, one by one.

Deane also sees the campaign as 'in some ways old-fashioned. We still did lots of paper-based stuff. We still had postcards that got mailed out. And we still had paper petitions and things like that. So, we did that in concert with social media, whereas these days I don't think anyone does the paper-based stuff at all anymore.'

The timing was just right. Facebook was all the rage, and was a great tool to spread the word. 'In the beginning, it was very much Facebook. And the website, which kept changing over time. The other thing that we did a lot of was to send out regular emails.'

Many people went to visit their local MP, to get them to support the NDIS. Nearly all of the 151 MPs in the House of Representatives received such a visit, most of them more than one. Baker says this blanket canvassing of MPs was another element that kept party politics out of the campaign.

Deane has a positive outlook, saying most MPs go into politics to make a difference. 'That might have been a long time ago, and they may have got distracted along the way, but go and remind them. And ask them to be your champion. They are used to having people come to them with complaints, but this is different—people coming to them with a great idea, saying, "Can you support this for me?"'

'I think those visits were powerful because so many politicians came to realise that they had never met a constituent who had a disability, which was something Jenny Macklin told me. Many visitors found the MP's office wasn't accessible. The website maintained a list of MPs who had received a visit—which meant you could see at a glance if your MP needed to be told.'

Della Bosca knew this side of the coin better than anyone.

'The other thing was that idea that people, when they're going to see their state or federal member, they're usually going with some grievance, they're going because they're angry about something, or something's wrong ... an immigration problem, or some other problem they want fixing. They very seldom go to their local member without a problem. So, members have all these people coming in and telling them about how everything is really crap and they hate everything, and there's all these problems lying on their desk all the time.

'We kind of developed this idea where we didn't want to do that. We will get up a bunch of people—sometimes they'll be carers, but sometimes they'll be people with disability. We'll get a group of them and try to cover every federal backbencher they can, of every political party, and get them to come from the electorate, and ten, twelve—or even fifteen, if we can get them—go along to the federal member's office and say, "Here's our cause—will you be our champion?" Not turning up to the member's office and whingeing about the disability system and everything else, instead saying, "We want to recruit you. We want to have a positive relationship with you."

'And what we found was that federal members fell over themselves wanting to be photographed with NDIS signs, which we then started putting up on the website. And it was quite interesting because eventually they realised that what we were doing was basically having a public commitment from every backbencher, of both political parties, to the scheme. And it was in perpetuity on the internet, so they couldn't get out of it. So, when it came to be contested in the parliament, they'd already been committed publicly.'

Shorten's idea to go outside Canberra, persuade everyone else first, and circle back to the capital was working perfectly. It was a reversal of how big policy changes usually work—it takes years for governments to persuade the public about a good, big idea before it can be accepted. This time, it was the population persuading the politicians, one by one, at local electoral offices.

Della Bosca kept his eye on polling, which showed support for the scheme increasing. 'Fundamentally, the idea of a public affairs campaign is to change the public's mind; what you aren't doing is lobbying. We didn't have a lobbyist in this campaign. I never went to see a politician. We trained people with disability to go and do the talking. And that really worked very well.'

Rob White agrees. 'The funding came from providers, but it was advocates and people with disabilities and their families who did the campaigning. Those families—Bill made us aware of the numbers, the number of people with disabilities, their parents, partners, siblings, you get to big numbers pretty quickly—they were the people power. The passion of the sector is my outstanding memory of the campaign.'

Says Deane: 'The campaign was ordinary folks who in other circumstances would never have dreamed of going to see their local MP. They didn't have anyone holding their hands to get out and see their MPs, they did it themselves.'

People did it all themselves.

They handed out leaflets at train stations in the morning.

They rang in to radio stations to have their say.

They posted videos on YouTube.

They put stickers on their cars.

They were turning invisibility into visibility.

Their messaging was clear and simple: help us by supporting the NDIS.

When people said, 'The NDIS is like Medicare for people with disability,' the message got straight through. The website and materials referenced the green Medicare card, reinforcing the point.

Says Della Bosca: 'The main catchcry was that anyone could become disabled at any time, and so there should be a scheme that provides for support services should such an incident occur.'

The actual Every Australian Counts team was very small. It was three full-time staff—Della Bosca, James O'Brien, Daniel Kyriacou; and three part-time staff—Fiona Anderson, Geraldine Mallett and Deane. They organised forums far and wide—from Cairns to Hobart to Perth—with speakers such as Bruce Bonyhady explaining the idea of the NDIS and how it would work. There were more than seventy consultations, thirty-five forums and eighteen roundtables held in every state and territory.

Slowly but surely, word spread. More professional bodies and organisations signed on with their support. Celebrities got involved. Ken Baker and Tim Walton, president of National Disability Services, got Sydney radio host Alan Jones on board and he ended up MCing a rally at the Opera House. The general populace was coming to a realisation that people with disability were getting a raw deal, and it had to be fixed.

The campaign was also affecting the politicians, who would eventually have to vote on the matter. When they talked among themselves, it quickly dawned on them that this thing was big. It affected everyone. It reminded Shorten of the days when Kevin Rudd was having his ministers hold community cabinet meetings in town halls. Inevitably, Shorten would get questions from the floor on disability, with more questions on that than on any other topic. Politicians simply hadn't twigged before to how big this problem was.

Bonyhady was incredibly impressed with the campaign and is in no doubt of the huge role it played in getting the NDIS accepted. 'The Every Australian Counts campaign just escalated and more than 150 000 people signed up, and members of parliament on all sides, sports stars, many people, were standing up in support,' he says. 'The conceptualisation of the NDIS was very clear, as a game changer, but perhaps at that stage everyone had a different practical understanding of what it would be. The known facts were that this scheme was portable—before the NDIS, if you moved from one state to another, the funding did not move with you; that it was going to be based on need; that it was not means-tested; and that it was going to meet the additional costs of disability, and wasn't capped. These facts were all very clear. I personally felt a huge sense of responsibility because what we were doing was, that we were selling something to a sector where there had been no hope and, in giving people hope, we had to deliver for them, because failure would have been devastating.

'People with disability and their families were out there telling their stories with enormous authenticity. It was people giving voice to their lived experience, which spoke so much more eloquently and effectively.

'It was a very low-cost campaign. We could not compete with the funding that the mining companies were throwing into their campaign against the mining tax. What we had were people and their authenticity, and we had hope. That's what we used. Their stories shocked Australians, because it's not how we like to think about ourselves.'

In looking back over the course of events, Bonyhady sees the NDIS starting as a welfare idea; being turned into a social policy idea and a human rights issue; being buttressed by becoming an economic notion; and, finally, becoming a political matter. 'For example, before key COAG [Council of Australian Governments meetings, when the federal government would meet state governments as the idea progressed], 6000 emails would be sent by members to the prime minister and premiers, asking them to support the NDIS. It would not have been possible to run that campaign without the use of technology and the power of the internet; we'd be still licking the stamps! It was a real grassroots campaign.'

Della Bosca also zeroed in on the patriotism angle in another way. The campaign repeatedly pointed out that on all international measures when calculating disability outcomes, Australia fared poorly. 'Australians have got the old cringe and always feel embarrassed about their performance internationally; like, "Are we doing better or worse than other people?" And what we could do was we could pick out the OECD figures about disability—we could point to the fact that of the twenty-three OECD nations that measure the relationship between poverty and disability, Australia was the third-worst performer, just before Mexico and Turkey,' he says.

Jenny Macklin has seen more campaigns than others have had hot breakfasts. She is in no doubt about the importance of Every Australian Counts. 'The Alliance created the Every Australian Counts campaign— the best grassroots campaign I have ever seen,' she says.

'We knew we had to go much further to build a case for change of the magnitude of the NDIS. We needed to walk what I know in politics is a very, very fine line. You do need to empower people by making them understand how broken the old system is, without frightening them so much that the problem seems too costly or too complicated to solve. On the other hand, fall on the wrong side of that line and your cabinet colleagues might decide that their priorities are much more important than yours and figure out ways to knock off what you've been delivering. I was very aware of those dangers.'

Jan McLucas remembers it well. 'While we in government were beavering away to develop stuff, that was when the three players—people with disability, carers and the service side—realised that they had to really have one voice. Every Australian Counts is as important as the Productivity Commission report, in terms of achieving what we did.

'You know, everybody just really joined into Every Australian Counts and then it became not just something about those "poor people". It was a community responsibility. And we had those massive rallies and walking across bridges; we had the Every Australian Counts website and Twitter and all that, and it became a community campaign, not just a campaign for people who sit in wheelchairs. It was fantastic to be part of; it was really humbling to be in the government that was trying to achieve this thing when you knew you had millions and millions of people who were supporting the goal.'

Rhonda Galbally had succeeded. As she puts it, 'The Alliance became strong enough to fuel the successful campaign for the NDIS: the Every Australian Counts Campaign. This campaign led to massive community mobilisation, which in turn led to almost unheard of bipartisan support ... It really is a miracle that it came together, considering the very different views, from the different interests represented, of what the NDIS would bring. The NDIS captured the imagination of every stakeholder in the disability sector—families, people with disabilities, and services. Everyone was united in campaigning for Every Australian Counts.'

The campaign changed John Della Bosca's mind in one respect—Australians really did believe in a fair go. 'Showing people that things were unfair to people with disabilities and showing them that there was something that could be done about it—you know, the public mind-set just changed completely.'

'UNDERFUNDED, UNFAIR, FRAGMENTED, INEFFICIENT'

———

EVERYONE IN THE Great Hall of Parliament House at the Disability Awards night in 2009 was thrilled when prime minister Kevin Rudd announced that the government would push ahead with a thorough examination of the feasibility of a National Disability Insurance Scheme.

They were even happier when they read the terms of reference.

'While Australia's social security and universal health care systems provide an entitlement to services based on need, there is currently no equivalent entitlement to disability care and support services,' it stated.

At last, people thought, *Our rights are actually being recognised—and acted upon.*

'The Government is committed to finding the best solutions to improve care and support services for people with disability. An exploration of alternative approaches to funding and delivering disability services with a focus on early intervention and long-term care will be an important contribution to the National Disability Strategy.'

At last, they thought, *that's what we need: early intervention, long-term planning, and it's national—so no more problems with portability, no more blame-shifting between governments.*

Even better—the model to be examined was based on an insurance one. It would be no-fault, universal and not means-tested.

The inquiry would be into a scheme that 'replaces the existing system ... ensures a range of support options is available, including individualised approaches, includes a coordinated package of care services which could include accommodation support, aids and equipment, respite, transport and a range of community participation and day programs available for a person's lifetime, and assists the person with disability to make decisions about their support.'

My god, they thought, *this is everything we have been asking for*. People could barely believe what they were reading.

But trepidation set in the moment everyone heard who would conduct the inquiry: the Productivity Commission. Their hopes had been dashed so often—now they lay in the hands of hard-headed economists, who did not necessarily have any understanding of disability.

The Productivity Commission was established in 1998. Its predecessor was the Industries Assistance Commission (IAC), set up by the Whitlam government in 1973. That had grown out of the Tariff Board, which started in 1921, and advised on taxes and tariffs on goods traded internationally, setting borders to promote Australia's economic interests. Whitlam's IAC had a wider remit. It advised, as the name suggests, on assistance to industry more generally, beyond tariffs and taxes, while also taking into consideration the consumer, as opposed to the worker or the business. It was tweaked in 1989 by the Hawke government, to give it a focus on reducing regulation.

The Productivity Commission has a wider purview still, its goal being the encouragement of a more efficient and productive economy. In short, it examines ideas to see if they are good for the nation. As the commission puts it, 'Our role, expressed most simply, is to help governments make better policies, in the long-term interest of the Australian community.'

Over the years, it has been staffed by people from business, the public service and academia, many of them at the top of their fields. The commission is independent, in that government directs it to investigate topics and it finds what it may; is transparent, in that its reports are made public; and has a community-wide focus, meaning that it examines the likely side effects of its recommendations, not just the effect within the immediate narrow field of inquiry.

The commission is anti-protectionist and pro-competition, which earns it the label 'economic rationalist', or 'neoconservative', or 'neoliberal'—none of which ideologies is traditionally supportive of welfare. Which is why disability advocates were wary of the commission. But, again, the idea it was examining, a national disability insurance scheme, is not welfare—it's insurance.

Bruce Bonyhady, an economist himself, registered others' concerns. 'What would these economic rationalists think about disability insurance? They could have completely panned it,' he later said.

DIG chairman Ian Silk remembers the feeling. 'There was a level of apprehension amongst the members of the DIG about the government's choice of the Productivity Commission to undertake that work. The apprehension was because the Productivity Commission was seen in some quarters as pointy-headed economists who wouldn't see the social benefits and the broader community benefits of an NDIS. The apprehension was that they'd look at the dollars, be very conservative in their assumptions [and] that would inevitably take them to a point that the NDIS was not a goer.'

Labor senator Jan McLucas felt the same way. 'I was initially concerned about that. I just thought the PC was too much of an economics body.'

But Jenny Macklin and Bill Shorten knew best. If the Productivity Commission said yes, then in all likelihood the NDIS would happen. If the Productivity Commission said no, then in all likelihood it wasn't a workable proposition anyway. The DIG report, however, gave the government enough confidence to proceed. In a sense, there was nothing to lose.

'Disability people really didn't want the Productivity Commission to do the work,' Macklin says. 'I had to convince them this was the best way to go, otherwise it wouldn't happen.'

'I took the submission to cabinet for the Productivity Commission to examine this,' she recalls. 'If Rudd had opposed it, it wouldn't have happened. It's important to give him that credit.'

When Shorten argued his case to cabinet, it was precisely the Productivity Commission's imprimatur that he sought. 'I agitated and agitated, I put together a submission, and presented it to cabinet. I wanted the Productivity Commission. I wanted people to think of disability not just as a cost, but as a benefit.

'The unique nature of this idea is that it's a left–right idea. Left, in that it's a generous safety net; right, in that individuals control it, not charities or the public service.'

One person who wasn't overly concerned was Ara Cresswell, from Carers Australia. 'The Productivity Commission has done extraordinary things over the years,' she says, adding, 'Beancounters have hearts too.'

Then there was more good news: John Walsh would be an associate commissioner on the inquiry. He knew better than anyone the inner details of how such a scheme could work. 'I wanted the Productivity Commission,' says Shorten, 'and I also wanted to pick the commissioner and have an advisory panel. Got John Walsh on it; that made all the difference.'

Walsh had done the foundational work on DIG, and much, much more.

As mentioned, he was Australia's Actuary of the Year in 2001. After his accident playing rugby league for Newton Bluebags, he could not pursue his pure maths honours degree at the University of Sydney and his desire to be an astrophysicist, because the old university simply could not accommodate his needs. Thanks to the intervention of a doctor, he began a cadetship as an actuary. Instead of looking far into the past, he would be looking far into the future. It was a five-year course that took Walsh ten years because of the difficulties imposed on him.

After a study tour of the United Kingdom, United States and Canada, he returned to Australia. He began to collate data on spinal cord injuries, which meant going to spinal units in hospitals and convincing them to hand over the information. The state of data collection was that poor, but Walsh began the process of improving it. The result was the Australian Spinal Cord Injury Register.

Walsh knew of the Whitlam legislation and the Woodhouse report—'that's how I began thinking about all this'—and ended up reviewing the New Zealand scheme, which had been legislated back in 1972. He worked at PwC, and became the actuary for the New South Wales WorkCover scheme and motor accident insurance scheme, and for South Australia's, too. He met weekly with the New South Wales minister, John Della Bosca, about the state's WorkCover compensation scheme. When Della Bosca then became the minister for disability, he asked Walsh to survey the data on New South Wales' disability services. What he found was 'scary'—cost increases of 7 to 10 per cent above inflation for the foreseeable future. The result was Stronger Together: a massive injection of more than $1 billion to stabilise that system into the future. Walsh was also instrumental in transforming New South Wales' motor scheme into a lifetime care and support scheme in 2006.

In 2005 Walsh wrote the so-called Blue Book, which grew out of the Ipp review into civil liability in the 1990s. The Blue Book sought to standardise the various state no-fault motor accident compensation schemes; extend them nationally; turn them into long-term care schemes rather than lump-sum schemes; and make them cover medical negligence, sport accidents, domestic accidents, and injuries as a result of assault (that is, cover all cases where courts offered no compensation). Before the 2007 election, he met with Ken Henry, head of treasury, and Jeff Harmer, head of FaHCSIA, who were enthusiastic about the proposals. That scheme was to be the National Injury Insurance Scheme—which the country is still waiting for.

After Labor's election win in 2007, Shorten, who knew of this proposed scheme, went to Sydney and met Walsh, the go-to man in this field, straightaway. They talked about the long-term scheme for the catastrophically injured.

While part of Shorten's DIG, Walsh was asked whether the scheme could be extended to disability. He said yes, what you need is the data, from which you project the costs, from which you deduce what the premiums have to be to cover the costs. DIG did the costings and concluded such a scheme was feasible. Now, Walsh and the Productivity Commission were going to do a deeper dive.

It was not unprecedented to have an associate commissioner appointed to the Productivity Commission in this way, but it was rare. Nor was it easily achieved.

'Bill [Shorten] called me again in probably around mid-2009 and said he wanted me to go on the Productivity Commission and do the work on what became the NDIS,' Walsh recalls. 'It wasn't a simple matter to get the Productivity Commission to agree to get me coming on board. I had to meet with Gary Banks [the commission chairman] and convince him I was legit. I got on well with Gary.'

Walsh already knew Patricia Scott, who would be the lead commissioner—in the end, the only other commissioner. 'I'd actually met Patricia before this, in her role as secretary of the department of human services. I was a PwC consultant coming in to meet a client—the department secretary. Patricia was tough. She was as hard as nails. At the PC, Patricia was as nice to me as she could possibly have been. She didn't know much about disability, but she was happy to acknowledge that. So I had pretty much free rein, and she was happy for me to take the running and lead them along the path.'

There was yet more good news for the sector: the commission would have a panel advising it that included disability advocates and those with lived experience of disability. It was rare to have an associate commissioner appointed, but it was unprecedented for the commission to have an advisory panel attached. And the good news just kept getting better: Bruce Bonyhady, Rhonda Galbally and Ian Silk, among others, would be advising the commission.

This came about partly at the insistence of Galbally.

As we saw earlier, the sector was resistant to the commission carrying out the inquiry. Macklin says, 'So they said, "If that's the case, we'd like an advisory panel." Treasury asked the Productivity Commission about it, and they agreed. Commissioner Patricia Scott—she really was fantastic. It was a great thing that they agreed to have this advisory board. Having the calibre of those people helped. And, of course, John Walsh as an associate commissioner.' This was the outcome that Shorten had argued for before cabinet.

There was still trepidation among the sector, though—would the advisory panel be listened to? Would the Productivity Commission resent its existence?

Ian Silk is more than happy to admit that the fear of the Productivity Commission was unfounded. 'The apprehension, I'm pleased to say, was poorly conceived, because the very reason a number of us were apprehensive was precisely the reason why it was a good idea to have them do it. Automatically, it [the inquiry] then had an air of credibility to it. If you sent it off to people who might be described as bleeding hearts, and they said it was a good idea, people would shrug their shoulders and say, "Well, of course they did. Why don't we get some serious folk to have a look at it?"'

He was also happy with how the commission and the advisory panel worked together. 'I recall in the initial discussion with the advisory panel that they were pushing back quite hard, but in a very fair and objective fashion, about some of the assumptions in the PwC work and the work we had undertaken. They were being rigorous and robust in their analysis.

'They, the Productivity Commission, didn't betray any resistance. It was very clear this was a Productivity Commission exercise, not a joint exercise with the panel. But they had nothing to lose. If I was them, I'd think, "I have access to these people, some of whom, like Rhonda, are deep experts in their field, and I can take on board all, some or none of what they say, but I have nothing to lose. There's no downside for me here." We didn't get any sense that they were there [meeting with us] reluctantly. Instead, the people chosen at the Productivity Commission to undertake the work became very strong advocates.

'There was no encroachment on their turf, because we were just responding, providing information in good faith, but it was always understood by both parties that they were running this race.'

The commission had the work of DIG and PwC at its disposal, but did its own. Walsh agrees that the work that had already been done provided a good starting point, even if there was a lot more to do.

Ian Silk again: 'They weren't bringing us slabs of text and saying, "Have a read of this, give us your thoughts. They were really running their own exercise. It wasn't a peer review of the work that PwC had undertaken. They went back and effectively started from scratch. They would occasionally bring new questions to us, questions that had occurred in their thinking; or they would often do some work and then say, "We think that A, B, C might be the case, but in your work, you thought X, Y, Z might be the case. Explain to us how you came to X, Y, Z." So, there were some exchanges like that, including assumptions around take-up rates. And that was a lot of work that the actuaries at PwC had done that [had] since been tested by our group at DIG.

'The panel usually met en masse with the people from the Productivity Commission. There may have been bilateral exchanges, individual to individual, but we met a number of times in a joint forum. It was apparent towards the end of our interaction that Commissioner Patricia Scott thought this was an idea with real merit. She was the lead commissioner, that was pretty important.'

Jan McLucas is someone else quite prepared to concede her misgivings about the commission were misplaced. 'I was wrong. Absolutely wrong,' she says.

The Productivity Commission conducted its own research, by a team that numbered as many as twenty people. The result was a two-volume report that came in at just under 1000 pages (more, if you count the sixty-nine pages of references).

The commission also conducted public hearings. Walsh was at them all—and heard what he expected to hear about a broken system. Once more, people with disability and their carers came out in droves to testify.

'People were desperate,' he says. 'We heard stories about parents who effectively committed a murder/suicide rather than relinquish their child to state group homes and state care.'

One submission from a psychiatrist, ultimately published prominently in the Productivity Commission's report, said, 'The regularity with which I meet parents with murder/suicide ideation as they have been unable to find adequate help for their child is both alarming, but also a marker of the failure of coordination of any service ... I also note that murder/suicide in these families is becoming a more recognised event, as recently occurred in Victoria.'

The commission heard from a woman in a wheelchair who said that the extent of her disability entitled her to have someone come and help her have three showers a week instead of two. Rendered incontinent as a result of the accident that had incapacitated her, she had to sit in her urine, in Brisbane heat, the other four days.

'I remember her. I can see her in my mind's eye,' says Walsh, more than a decade later. 'She was pretty emotional, very upset about the treatment she was receiving.' It was even more confronting for Commissioner Scott.

Bruce Bonyhady believes that woman made a significant impression on the lead commissioner. 'Can you imagine sitting there in Brisbane in the heat of summer in your own urine, four days a week? When she presented to the Productivity Commission, she told how the strain of getting to that hearing had made her vomit. She … said that before her injury, she had worked in the commonwealth public service for the presiding commissioner. The impact on Patricia when she realised that this woman had worked for her, and this is what had happened—I think this had a personal impact on her.'

Rhonda Galbally is likewise full of praise for Commissioner Scott. 'She was a seasoned head of many government departments, who might have been expected to have seen it all,' she wrote in her book *Just Passions*. 'But she hadn't. Patricia was truly outraged by the absolute chaos in disability; she was outraged by the unfairness of the system and by the tragedy of the lives wasted from unmet need.'

Kirsten Deane attended some of the hearings. 'I remember one in Melbourne, in particular, where a lovely man who I subsequently got to know brought his son along. And his son, who … was non-verbal wrote beautiful poetry. And this man talked about his son's life and then read some things that his son wanted. They'd worked it out before, what his son wanted to say. Now, that's totally not your usual Productivity Commission hearing. But that was exactly the kind of stories that actually made such an impact on the commission.'

Emotional stories, of course, would not be enough to convince the Productivity Commission—but it did listen to them, and they did have an impact.

∽

The beauty of the NDIS as conceived at the start, then seconded and expanded in the DIG report, was that it wiped out at a stroke many of the difficulties in the system that people had been complaining about for decades, and that were still being reported in these hearings.

It eliminated the system's opaqueness that meant it was impossible even to find out what services were available.

It removed the difficulty and administrative burden of having to apply for multiple services, and renew applications, year in, year out.

It removed the dreadful uncertainty—the misery lottery—of whether your application would succeed.

It eased the minds of parents who feared their own deaths, not knowing their child's fate; it eased the mind of the child too.

It did away with the barrier to moving interstate.

It wiped out the bureaucratic nightmare of losing some benefits or services if you gained others, of being ineligible for service A if you were in system B.

It lifted hidden barriers to work.

It ended the cruelty of your rights being extinguished at the moment the relevant budget ran out.

It would plug the holes in the knowledge base, by gathering the necessary data and applying sophisticated modelling to it.

It was national, removing the inequity of different state systems offering different levels of support.

It put the person with disability at the centre, enabling individual choice, which meant empowerment.

It responded to needs as they changed, introducing the flexibility that was so severely lacking.

It was lifelong—and that brought certainty, which relieved the constant grinding stress of wondering if the services you needed would continue into the future.

It provided the early intervention and investment that are the hallmark of an insurance scheme—reducing long-term costs and bringing with it discipline, security and transparency, while also investing the premiums to provide funds into the future.

DIG, of course, took the view that trying to reform the system as it stood was a lost cause. Doing so would simply lock in the failures that had bedevilled the lives of so many for so long.

Most of all, the NDIS would save money in the long run. It would lower costs elsewhere, across government, as well as providing better outcomes, lives of opportunity and dignity.

The beauty of the report that was handed down by the Productivity Commission on 31 July 2011—after eighteen months of excruciating examination, of intense testing of the theory against the most extensive data, of extraordinarily detailed costings and projections of future needs, of sober consideration, after hearing more than 1000 submissions—was that it recommended just such a National Disability Insurance Scheme.

~

'The current disability support system is underfunded, unfair, fragmented, and inefficient, and gives people with a disability little choice and no certainty of access to appropriate supports. The stresses on the system are growing, with rising costs for all governments,' commissioners Scott and Walsh declared in their report.

'Most families and individuals cannot adequately prepare for the risk and financial impact of significant disability. The costs of lifetime care can be so substantial that the risks and costs need to be pooled.

'There should be a new national scheme—the National Disability Insurance Scheme (NDIS)—that provides insurance cover for all Australians in the event of significant disability. Funding of the scheme should be a core function of government (just like Medicare).

'The main function of the NDIS would be to fund long-term high quality care and support (but not income replacement) for people with significant disabilities. Everyone would be insured and around 410 000 people would receive scheme funding support.'

So said the Productivity Commission.

'It's not mealy-mouthed bureaucratese, is it,' says Ian Silk. 'It's quite a stake in the ground, a definitive document that says, "This is a goer" or "This can be a goer."'

'If we, DIG, hadn't made our recommendation, the NDIS would have died there and then. So that was a necessary but far from sufficient condition [for it to advance]. But when the PC came back with their view so clearly stated to the government—which was disposed to an NDIS but had not formally committed to it—I thought the PC report would give them sufficient confidence that they could proceed with it.'

This PC report did what no other had ever done: it made people cry. The hopes, the needs, of people with disability and their carers might finally be met.

The report moved on to the problems as the commission saw them. It confirmed what people had been saying for decades.

'The existing disability support "system" is unsustainable on multiple grounds,' it said.

It confirmed the system was driven by crisis: 'It is becoming increasingly unstable. The high costs of addressing people with crisis needs impede funding for other support services. This is because when faced with budget constraints, systems have little choice but to give priority to families in crisis. This displaces funds for early intervention and respite programs, increasing further the number of families falling into crisis, and leading to an ongoing causal relationship between shortages and crises.'

It confirmed that the demographics condemned the system to failure, and greater failure, as time went on: 'Another contributor to the pressure on existing arrangements is that people with disabilities are living longer, and at some point can no longer be supported by their ageing parents or partners. Eventually this cycle must either absorb more and more funds, or leave people in increasingly abhorrent conditions.'

It confirmed that funding was insufficient, and that this increased costs in the long run: 'There is not sufficient resourcing, with many gaps in services in all jurisdictions and most locations. Rationing is likely to get worse unless there is reform. Rationing places an unreasonable burden on people with a disability and their families. It means lower levels of wellbeing and large forgone life chances. There are particularly big gaps in the availability of support at key transition points in people's lives. People wait years for specialist wheelchairs, need to stay with their parents instead of moving into independent supported accommodation, and do not get timely or sufficient access to support.'

It confirmed that the system was also destroying the lives of carers: 'Carers have among the lowest levels of wellbeing of any group of Australians.'

It confirmed all the complaints about uncertainty: 'People with disabilities and their carers do not get the certainty of lifelong support needed for proper life planning and cannot avoid the extreme anxiety about the adequacy of future funded support when informal care is no longer reasonable or feasible. Current funding for disability comes from two levels of government, which are subject to annual budget cycles—making it hard to give people with disabilities any certainty that they will get reasonable care and support over the long run.'

It confirmed that those already disadvantaged were disadvantaged all over again: 'Inadequate services can hit certain communities particularly hard—such as people in regional and remote areas, people from a non-English speaking background and Indigenous people.'

It confirmed that uncoordinated spending made things worse: 'Under-servicing in one area—such as not enough access to respite and home modifications—results in costly additional servicing in another less appropriate area or at a later time (such as someone staying in hospital because their home has not been modified).'

It confirmed that people without choices were disempowered: 'People with a disability have too little control over what happens to them and limited choice of service providers. The usual justification for such paternalism—the complexity of services—has little application in a sector where one of the most important services is relatively straightforward personal support in which the empathy and responsiveness of the carer is the most important feature.'

It confirmed that disability services were barely obtainable even when available: 'The "system" is hard to navigate (a "confusopoly" in the words of one participant) and is not well integrated nationally. Even within a jurisdiction, people deal with a multitude of programs and agencies, few of which coordinate or share information. If people move across state boundaries, their entitlements can stop at the border.'

It confirmed that the 'system' came first, the person second: 'People are told they must fit the programs—rather than have programs meet their needs—with wasteful effort going into manoeuvring around the rules. Some people fall inevitably through the cracks, notwithstanding administrators accepting that their reasonable needs are not being met.'

Then it moved to the all-important question, the question everyone dreaded: cost. Before considering cost, it was imperative to consider what the cost would be if nothing was done: 'The cost of doing nothing would be the persistence and increasing intensity of the above deficiencies. Moreover, governments could not feasibly do absolutely nothing. They would need to patch up their systems to arrest the vicious cycle produced by systems in crisis. In effect, all governments face future liabilities with their current unstable systems. The implication of this is that the upfront *fiscal* costs, while significant, are partly offset by eliminating the hidden future liabilities of the current system. Moreover, from an *economic* perspective, the benefits of the NDIS will exceed the costs.'

That was a conclusion few were expecting.

It moved then to actual cost: 'Current funding for disability is subject to the vagaries of governments' budget cycles. People with disabilities have no certainty that they will get reasonable care and support over the long run. Resourcing might be good one year, but insufficient the next, with many people missing out. The Commission estimates that the amount needed to provide people with the necessary supports would be about double current spending (an *additional* $6.5 billion per annum).'

From there, it moved to cost/benefit analysis: 'The benefits of the scheme would significantly outweigh the costs. The NDIS would only have to produce an annual gain of $3800 per participant to meet a cost-benefit test. Given the scope of the benefits, that test would be passed easily.'

Then to the social benefit: 'People would know that, if they or a member of their family acquired a significant disability, there would be a properly financed, comprehensive, cohesive system to support them.'

From there to how it would be funded: 'The Commission proposes several options for providing certainty of future funding. Its preferred option is that the Australian Government should finance the entire costs of the NDIS by directing payments from consolidated revenue into a National Disability Insurance Premium Fund, using an agreed formula entrenched in legislation. The amount needed could be funded through a combination of cuts in existing lower-priority expenditure, fiscal drag [where inflation pushes taxpayers into higher tax brackets], and if necessary, tax increases.'

Then to what this NDIS would do: 'The scheme should involve a common set of eligibility criteria, entitlements to individually tailored supports based on the same assessment process, certainty of funding based on need, genuine choice over how their needs were met (including choice of provider) and portability of entitlements across borders. There would be local area coordinators and disability support organisations to provide grassroots support. The insurance scheme would take a long-term view and have a strong incentive to fund cost-effective early interventions, and collect data to monitor outcomes and ensure efficiency.'

And then to who it would be for: 'The NDIS is for all Australians.'

It defined all Australians as Tier 1. Anyone with or affected by disability was Tier 2, and could approach the NDIS for information about care and support options. Then there was Tier 3, 'targeted at the much smaller group of people with significant care and support needs,' to whom individualised packages would be available.

After 987 pages, the report concluded: 'Drawing on the above evidence, the Commission considers that the benefits of the NDIS would significantly exceed the additional costs of the scheme.'

The Productivity Commission had examined everything that people with disability had been asking for. It decided, on the basis of what was good for the country and good for the economy, that they should have what they had been asking for.

~

Prime Minister Gillard hosted a meeting at the Lodge of the key players. Jenny Macklin, Bill Shorten and Jan McLucas were all there, along with Bruce Bonyhady, John Walsh, Rhonda Galbally, Ian Silk, Ann Sherry, a former public servant and businesswoman with lived experience of disability, and Kevin Cocks, a lifelong advocate and future Queensland anti-discrimination commissioner.

Kevin Rudd had been prime minister when the Productivity Commission was instructed to test the idea of the NDIS, and Shorten had had responsibility for disability services. Things had changed on 24 June 2010, when Gillard took the prime ministership. In the ministry she announced after the August 2010 election, Shorten became assistant treasurer and minister for financial services and superannuation, McLucas took his role in disability services, and Macklin took responsibility for the NDIS, ultimately becoming minister for disability reform. Shorten, however, maintained a keen interest throughout.

The exact nature of the dinner remains ambiguous: the final decision to go ahead had not been made, and Gillard wanted to hear from those with an interest in the NDIS. In a way, it's like the film *Rashomon*—everyone remembers the event quite differently.

It was a phones-off meeting, but with a degree of informality. McLucas recalls that 'Julia ran it as a meeting. She wanted all these people with views to tell us what we do next. It was going around the people, so all these people could have their say. I think there was a view that this would be the centrepiece of this government.'

Bill Shorten had asked Gillard for the meeting. 'I said to her, "I'll get the smartest people in the room to talk about disability."'

Ian Silk recalls the prime minister running the dinner. 'It was a serious matter that had brought everybody there,' he says. 'The atmosphere was a combination of serious interrogation of the issues and a restrained celebration, because the sense of it happening was very real. It was quite a subdued environment. I don't recall laughter or anything. The prime minister was leading the discussion, very clearly, asking questions, pushing back, probing. It was like a briefing in a business office, or a Parliament House office, but a dinner. When I walked out I remember speaking to Bruce and saying, "It's pretty clear the PM's on board." But there was no uncritical support—she wanted to be satisfied that this was going to work. At the end of the evening, she gave all the indications that it would work.'

Bruce Bonyhady: 'This dinner started with small talk, then it was called to order, and each of us got to talk about why the scheme was so important. I can't quite remember Julia's words, but it was so obvious that she had accepted our argument that we went back to small talk. We'd done our business. It didn't seem to take very long. Julia was obviously very warm to the idea, and she basically reassured us that it had her support. There's something else about that dinner that really stuck in my mind. There were two people at that table who were quadriplegics, and the food that was served meant that they could cut it themselves and eat the dinner without any assistance. I don't know who chose the menu for the night, but it was enabling—so hats off to them.'

There were no foodies in this lot. No one remembers what the actual meal was; nor did any have to hand their menu, which was given to guests to take home as a souvenir.

Jenny Macklin says the dinner was 'all part of building a case of "we need to do this". I don't think Julia needed persuading by that time. I think she was well down the path by then. It was good that everyone was there, but there was so much momentum [already] from so many people.'

Rhonda Galbally doesn't remember lobbying, as such (although she laughs at the memory of lobbying Gillard over dinner several years earlier, before she was PM, contrary to Galbally's partner's instructions). 'It was lovely to be asked,' she says. 'I thought Julia was pretty convinced and supportive by then. I thought it was more of a hosting of a dinner for those who had worked so hard. We did all have a say about it— I remember John Walsh speaking, and thinking, *He expresses that very well*. He was persuasive.'

John Walsh thinks the dinner was more than a thankyou: 'It was also, I think, to make sure things didn't fall over at the last hurdle. I remember particularly the Alliance of carers, people with disability and providers being urged to stay together. I would expect that what I would have said was "Don't forget that you need the right governance, systems and operational risk in place."'

There had also been another dinner.

In the middle of 2009, while DIG and PwC were testing the idea of the NDIS, John Walsh was helping with a review of New Zealand's Accident Compensation Corporation—the one set up as a result of the work of Sir Owen Woodhouse, who had so impressed Gough Whitlam.

Coincidentally, Bronwyn Morkham's Young People in Nursing Homes National Alliance was presenting at Labor's national conference, as part of its Fringe Program. The title of their presentation was 'It's Time'; the topic a national compensation scheme, just as her Alliance had submitted to the Senate disability inquiry in 2006. Her special guest: Sir Owen Woodhouse.

'We brought Sir Owen over from New Zealand in July 2009 to speak at the Labor Fringe Program,' Morkham recalls. Woodhouse had a special request: 'He asked me to see if he could catch up with Gough Whitlam.

'I got in contact with Whitlam's office, spoke to his private secretary, and there was this extraordinary meeting where these two men—giants, in my opinion—sat down. I didn't presume to be in the room, but I was invited, and a real privilege it was to see the two together again. The meeting was in Gough's office in Sydney.

'Both men were visionaries. I thanked Gough for enacting free education, telling him it enabled me to get through university. He turned to me and said, "It's funny you should say that. A lot of you young women tell me that." I thought *Good on you*.

'It was a really lovely opportunity to acknowledge Sir Owen and Gough. Both men were in their nineties. There was great affection between them, and great respect.

'The other thing we did when Sir Owen was in Sydney was to bring him together with some of the people who worked on his report for Gough at a dinner that PwC hosted.'

John Walsh was at that dinner. He, too, thinks fondly of the two men being reunited, regarding the occasion as 'very special'.

Ever the actuary, Walsh points out that Whitlam and Woodhouse were born within days of each other in 1916—11 July and 18 July respectively—and died within months of each other, ninety-eight years later.

'I have such admiration for those men for their vision,' Morkham says, still rankled by the Senate frustrating Whitlam's legislation in 1975. No matter—there would be something bigger around the corner.

NO TURNING BACK

―――

NOAH'S ARK IN Heidelberg, Melbourne was founded by parents of children with disability as a toy library in 1971, growing over the years to offer all sorts of programs and aids. On 10 August 2011 it played host to Prime Minister Julia Gillard, Jenny Macklin, Bill Shorten and Jan McLucas, plus many other familiar names, including Bruce Bonyhady, John Walsh, Rhonda Galbally, Kirsten Deane and Ken Baker. The prime minister had an announcement to make.

The government had decided to introduce the National Disability Insurance Scheme. It had done so virtually immediately upon receiving the Productivity Commission's report just two weeks earlier.

'The Productivity Commission has recommended that the nation move to a new model of funding disability,' Gillard said, 'a National Disability Insurance Scheme. It's sort of the same concept as Medicare. Medicare is the way in which we as a nation all come together and insure ourselves and each other against the risk of being unwell'—and the NDIS would do the same for those with a disability.

'I think it's an appropriate kind of fairness to say if someone met with a dreadful moment in their life, an accident, an illness, the birth of a child with a disability, that meeting with that moment, that chance in life, shouldn't cost them the ability to have a decent life. We don't want people left behind, and that's why I'm so enthusiastic to see us work towards a better way of looking after Australians with disabilities.'

Gillard acknowledged that the position of carers was precarious, and that people with disability were not getting the support they needed, while also emphasising that the scheme was for all Australians, any one of whom could become disabled at any moment.

She made a special point of thanking John Walsh, who had toiled over and tussled with the concept—and, perhaps more importantly, the data and the execution—for decades, culminating in his work with the Productivity Commission.

Bill Shorten also spoke. 'Impairment is a fact of life,' he said. 'It's what you do with the impairment which is what determines whether or not Australians have a second-class existence. We want to end the midnight anxiety of ageing carers who wonder who will look after their adult children when they no longer can. We want to end the second-class exile which too many Australians exist in. This is a reform not just for those who are catastrophically injured, but in fact for every Australian to have peace of mind.'

Macklin's eyes light up recalling that day. 'Julia decided she would announce in-principle support when the government released the Productivity Commission report. It was done in my electorate, so it was a very proud moment at Noah's Ark, in that great little toy library in Heidelberg Heights. It was a really special day.'

When asked whether Gillard took much persuading on the NDIS, Macklin has a succinct answer: 'No.' Shorten found the new PM, well known for her ability to get across a brief quickly and thoroughly, to be much more supportive of the idea than her predecessor had been.

'I think she could see this could be her signature reform,' Macklin says. 'From a social justice point of view, she could see we couldn't keep going on the way we were going. And, of course, the economics, which were so clearly set out in the Productivity Commission report. The states just couldn't afford it. And as Brian [Howe] and Bruce [Bonyhady] said right at the beginning, we needed a new way. We knew that we had to do a really substantial piece of policy.'

McLucas also remembers the prime minister's dedication.

'Julia became terribly engaged on this,' she says. 'She was fabulous. She got into the policy in an intellectual way, but also in an emotional way. For a woman with the tasks that she had in her government, it was beautiful to see. She totally got engaged.'

In her announcement, Gillard turned her attention to the work to come, which would be a 'long journey'. The commission had thought it would take seven years to get the full scheme running, taking into account everything required—a huge list, including strict criteria; a regulatory framework; staff; offices; building up expertise in many fields, including how to run an insurance scheme; computer systems; and, very importantly, a much-expanded service-providing workforce, which would need extensive training.

As the traditional providers of services, state governments would have to be involved, and so Gillard immediately proposed a select council as a forum to win agreement from them. An advisory committee was also announced, headed by senior public servant Jeff Harmer, with Bonyhady, Galbally and Baker on board.

Says McLucas: 'It was a huge thing to get this done—you had to get all the states involved. Then there was the question of the money. It was very difficult, all very difficult, but we did it.'

∽

And so, the work of turning a good idea—a good idea whose economic validity had been substantiated by the critical gaze of the Productivity Commission—into reality, began.

Macklin, the minister for disability reform since December 2011, had carriage of the project, which was never far from the attention of Prime Minister Gillard, her treasurer, Wayne Swan, and Bill Shorten, who was now in cabinet.

The meetings began. Bonyhady recalls just how things had changed at the time. Suddenly, everyone was on side. Instead of warning of the difficulties, the traps, the problems, the expense, it was all systems go, trying to make the NDIS work.

Gillard ran a minority government, which made everything difficult. It didn't stop her from being a very successful legislator—with 600 pieces of legislation passed—but made it harder, in that there usually had to be negotiations with the independents and the Greens. There was little reason to expect the Coalition to support the NDIS when it was opposing everything else. For eight months, opposition leader Tony Abbott prevaricated without saying no exactly, making noises about the budget.

To the surprise of many, he pledged his support in April 2012. He did so at an Every Australian Counts rally in Perth—and was cheered by the hundreds of attendees, decked out in their red campaign shirts.

Abbott referenced his nickname at the time, conferred on him for his relentless opposition: Dr No. 'When it comes to the National Disability Insurance Scheme, I am Dr Yes,' he told the crowd. 'We cannot allow ourselves to be distracted by the normal business of politics. We must make this a reality ... this will be done.'

Many have wondered why Abbott supported the NDIS. His position had been lukewarm, with him insisting on a budget surplus before full implementation.

That chimed with what his shadow treasurer, Joe Hockey, was saying more forcefully—no NDIS until there's a budget surplus. Which echoed what the previous Liberal treasurer, Peter Costello, was shouting from the sidelines: *we can't afford this*. Hockey's opposition was odd, given his former support for a national injury insurance scheme—which perhaps goes to show that his motivation in that case was the interests of small businesses and the cost of their insurance.

When the key players ponder the reasons for Abbott's support, they point, for starters, to Mitch Fifield, the shadow minister for disability. Fifield had privately expressed his support for the scheme to those in the field, even if he had been more circumspect in public. Fifield, however, had no business getting out ahead of his leader; once Abbott had backed it, though, he gave it full and unqualified support, especially at a National Disability Service forum in Adelaide that May.

The main players were in no doubt that Fifield was strongly recommending the scheme to Abbott, and fending off Hockey's criticism. If the nation had followed Hockey's prescription, we would still not have an NDIS. There has been just one budget surplus since—in 2022–23, with nothing but deficits tipped by treasury in the foreseeable future.

Bonyhady is happy to credit Abbott with understanding that the reform, beyond being equitable and a great thing for people with disability, was an economic reform for the nation's good.

Kirsten Deane has no trouble seeing the best in Abbott's decision to back the NDIS. 'Politicians usually become politicians because they want to make a difference,' she says. 'I think the decision is consistent with his ethos. I think he was persuaded by the argument that people with disability should have the same opportunity as everybody else. On the conservative side of politics, there is a preference for small government over big, and this was big government with a capital B and a capital G. But I think he could see this was about enabling people to have opportunity.'

Ken Baker sees a similar thing. 'I take this back to the issue of maintaining support across the spectrum. Built in within the NDIS concept are principles that do appeal to both sides of politics. It depends how you frame it. You can see it as a consumer rights issue, or you can emphasise that it's customer choice. If you describe it as customer choice, it has more appeal to the Liberal side. You can talk about it assisting the most disadvantaged, or you can talk about it as building people's capacity to be independent. The way it's framed has different appeals. And that's a good thing about this idea, that it can be framed to appeal to a broad spectrum.' All of which echoes Shorten's description of the scheme as a left–right idea.

Rhonda Galbally has a funny story to tell. She had bumped into Joe Hockey at an airport. Never backwards in coming forward—her wheelchair has no reverse gear—she badgered him on the NDIS and got a frosty response. Coincidentally, she shortly thereafter bumped into Abbott in Sydney, before he had announced his support. She had heard, however, that he was in favour. 'I said to him, "Mr Abbott, I'm hearing you're supporting the NDIS and I'm so pleased." And he said, "Well, normally I'm Mr No, but on this occasion I'm Mr Yes". And so I had a Press Club appearance and I quoted it. He then picked it up and said it everywhere. So it became his phrase!'

$\backsim$

The premiers ultimately agreed to the NDIS only days after the legislation was introduced—which obscures the fact that there were months and months of meetings beforehand with premiers, treasurers and bureaucrats, multiplied by six for each of the states, then again for each of the two territories. It was grinding work, like herding cats. Each premier wanted to get the best deal for their state; some of them wanted to gain any political mileage they could, while they were at it. Some thought it advisable to wait the longest to get the best deal; others could see an advantage in being the first to move. Some felt the pressure of their constituents wanting this thing and wanting it now; others, not so much. 'There was a lot of argy-bargy with the states about numbers, but that's normal,' says the phlegmatic Macklin, who was leading all this activity. 'I'm not pretending any of that work is glamorous—it's not glamorous—but it is the technical work that needs to be done.'

In a sense, the work was only just beginning.

'Once the in-principle decision was made by myself, the prime minister and the treasurer, then there was all that work,' she says. 'There are so many parts to a huge policymaking process. If I start from the end, there's the public servants who are doing all the negotiations to get the commonwealth–state agreements, to get the premiers to sign up. Ian Watt, who was the head of Prime Minister and Cabinet—a proper public servant—he gave all his best people to us. He did such an outstanding job to make it happen. The other woman who was very important who doesn't get much airplay was Helen Hambling. These huge reports don't just happen. Drafting the legislation, the cabinet submissions, the agreement with the states—we would not have an NDIS without the public service. Someone has to draft the legislation, someone has to write the submissions. There's all these people beavering away.

'There were all those meetings with premiers, treasurers, and the prime minister and Wayne Swan—you don't get there without very substantial work behind you.'

On 30 April 2012 Gillard and Macklin announced that the NDIS would launch in 2013, a year ahead of the Productivity Commission's timeline. The budget set aside $1 billion for that purpose. Politics played a part in the timing—the launch would be before an election, not after one. An election that was looking likely to be won by the opposition.

The launch sites were the carrot dangled before the premiers—there would not be a launch in every state, so the thinking was to inject a spirit of competition to get the premiers to sign up, lest they miss out. During the COAG meeting in July 2012, Gillard explained the politics of the situation, as she saw it, to the two Liberal premiers of the two biggest states, who were dragging their heels, Victoria's Ted Baillieu and New South Wales' Barry O'Farrell, who had been operating in unison.

In her book *My Story*, Gillard writes that O'Farrell was the quicker of the two to see the potential political problem in denying people with disability their NDIS launch site. The two finally agreed—which meant, given the agreements already reached with South Australia, Tasmania and the Australian Capital Territory, that this thing was going ahead. Queensland premier Campbell Newman would eventually have to sign up, even if he was complaining that his state, whose disability services were by far the most underfunded, had no money; as would Colin Barnett, premier of Western Australia, which had probably the best system and whose government wanted to ensure its people would be no worse off.

～

'Few actions in public life give me greater pleasure than introducing the National Disability Insurance Scheme bill does today.'

So said Prime Minister Gillard to parliament on 29 November 2012.

'The scheme to be established by this bill will transform the lives of people with disability, their families and carers. For the first time they will have their needs met in a way that truly supports them to live with choice and dignity. It will bring an end to the tragedy of services denied or delayed, and instead offer people with disability the care and support they need over their lifetimes. This is a complex bill, yet at its heart is a very simple moral insight: disability can affect any of us and therefore it affects all of us.'

Referencing not Whitlam's 'inequality of luck' but Ben Chifley's 'shards of fate', Gillard said disability could not be avoided, but its consequences—'isolation, poverty, loss of dignity, stress, hopelessness and fear of the future'—could be. And should be. And would be, under the NDIS.

'So today our nation says enough. Our current system is inadequate and indefensible. It must be replaced.'

And it would be replaced, the prime minister said, with something universal, because the 'risk of disability is universal'. The NDIS would respond to people's needs, not ration funds according to arbitrary budgets, which were 'a cruel lottery'.

She turned her attention to carers, 'required to stretch the bonds of obligation and kinship past breaking point'. She noted that the nation was being robbed of the human and economic potential of people with disability.

The NDIS was transformational, Gillard said—and while the current system remained, the nation was diminished.

'This bill will inscribe in our laws a substantial and enduring reform that will fundamentally change the nature of disability care and support in this nation: the National Disability Insurance Scheme,' she continued.

It would assess a person's needs and respond accordingly, giving that person choice and control regarding their supports, giving them the opportunity to manage their own funding, making them masters of their destiny.

People with disability would be cared for and/or supported for life, putting to an end the uncertainty and its attendant fear that marred and scarred so many lives.

The legislation observed the rights of people with disability, and would give effect to national obligations undertaken via the UN Convention. It promised early intervention, to minimise the effect of disability and maximise a person's potential.

Having outlined the major provisions, Gillard said her thankyous: 'to Productivity Commission commissioner Patricia Scott and Associate Commissioner John Walsh, for their thorough and compelling analysis that has been critical to the shape of the NDIS, to a remarkable story of advocacy, led by Bruce Bonyhady and Rhonda Galbally, the National Disability and Carer Alliance, the National People with Disabilities and Carer Council, and friends, activists and advocates in communities right across the country, to colleagues Jenny Macklin for her public policy genius in realising our vision for change, Bill Shorten for his passion for this cause as parliamentary secretary and his ongoing support, and Jan McLucas for her patient, caring and accessible approach in dealing with all who need to be heard.

'My distinguished predecessor Gough Whitlam sought to introduce a national compensation scheme forty years ago,' the prime minister said. 'Today, a new generation—no less idealistic—seeks to perfect and complete that work.

'For four years, this idea has grown from seed. Over the past year, we have built the foundations. Now this legislation will make the scheme real. The National Disability Insurance Scheme is the greatest change to Australian social policy in a generation and a mark of how deeply the conscience of our nation has been touched.

'The NDIS will stand alongside the minimum wage, the age pension, Medicare and universal superannuation as one of the great Labor pillars of social justice and opportunity for all Australians. It will change our society in profound and lasting ways, enabling those who live with disability to fulfil their potential as valued and valuable members of our society. I count it as a privilege to introduce this legislation today.'

When Gillard finished, her colleagues stood and cheered.

The day was the culmination of so much hard work, so much hope invested, for so many people. The Disability Awards had been held in Canberra just two nights earlier, and many attendees had stayed in town for this event.

Ken Baker was one, and he has a memento—a picture with Gillard, Macklin and Swan. 'The look of satisfaction and pleasure on their faces is quite something. It was a great day.'

Bronwyn Morkham, from the Young People in Nursing Homes National Alliance, was another, who likewise remembers a great day, with one shadow. 'I was in the House when Julia Gillard presented the bill for the NDIS. The gallery was full, the government benches were full, but there were only two people in the House on the opposition benches. Two. It was terrible to see the opposition benches so empty. It's hard to understand.' This left these people feeling snubbed, on the day the nation was extending its hand to them in a way it never had before. Rhonda Galbally was there too. 'That was a wonderful day,' she recalls, but also noting there were only two people on the opposition benches. 'That was a shock.' It was bewildering and made everyone doubt whether the so-called bipartisanship was real.

Jenny Macklin takes a more pragmatic view. 'If they didn't vote against it, then they voted for it. I think it should be said they all supported it.'

Bill Shorten agrees that the key issue was their votes, 'but with the hindsight of eleven years, and even at the time, it was exceedingly poor judgement. It was a byproduct of the toxic atmosphere at the time and the extraordinary partisanship against Gillard.' As for how he felt on the historic day, it's simple: 'I was rapt.'

❧

The nation was getting an NDIS but, of course, that didn't mean all the work was done. From the House of Representatives, the legislation passed to the Senate, which, in turn, referred it to the Community Affairs Legislation Committee.

The committee then did its work, which involved eleven more public hearings across the country, and a further 1600 submissions. Once again, many of them were made by the people who mattered most—those with disability. The committee had a deadline of 13 March 2013, and it reported back with twenty-nine recommendations.

So it was that the legislation returned to the House of Representatives and, on the morning of 21 March 2013, became the law of the land.

Cracks, however, were beginning to appear.

John Walsh, who had done so much, first on DIG then with the Productivity Commission, had severe misgivings. He was worried about the rushed introduction, a year before the commission had recommended it occur. He was very worried about the fleeting reference to actuarial and insurance principles within the legislation—if such principles were not followed, the consequences would be crushing. He was most concerned by the fact that while the parent body, the National Disability Insurance Agency, was independent, the NDIS was a department portfolio. He thought it, too, should be independent, and reporting quarterly and annually to a specialist, dedicated unit in treasury, the only department that had the expertise to monitor the financials. Such reports should identify risks, 'particularly in regard to the capacity of the expected funding stream to meet expected demand ... the source of the risks and the adequacy of strategies to address those risks'. He wrote to the prime minister's office with his concerns, but received no reply.

Walsh was also concerned, as was Morkham, that work had stalled on the National Injury Insurance Scheme (NIIS), for those disabled because of injury. Being much smaller, the NIIS was supposed to precede the full NDIS and provide an evidentiary and practical base for it. The NIIS was meant to provide rehabilitation for the injured, which was not covered by the NDIS as rehab was a matter for health departments. This also left a gaping loophole: the NDIS only admitted people under sixty-five, which meant injured people over sixty-five were still not covered.

Nevertheless, the day had come—and what a day it was.

After passing the legislation in the morning, Prime Minister Gillard had an apology to make—making her day rather like the day Jenny Macklin had when Bonyhady and Brian Howe came to see her in her office after that other Apology.

This apology was to the children who between 1945 and 1973 had been forcibly adopted, and to their mothers, and even their fathers. The apology was because the government did not provide single mothers with the benefits that went to widows and deserted wives.

'Today this Parliament, on behalf of the Australian people, takes responsibility and apologises for the policies and practices that forced the separation of mothers from their babies, which created a lifelong legacy of pain and suffering,' Gillard told the 800-strong audience in Parliament's Great Hall. Among that audience, in one of the front few rows, sat Paul Howes, national secretary of the Australian Workers' Union. He had been adopted. He was crying. He was Gillard's friend.

Howes had not always been her friend—he had opposed the move by Gillard and Kevin Rudd to depose Kim Beazley and Jenny Macklin in 2006. But as they worked together to replace the WorkChoices legislation, they had bonded. When Gillard challenged Rudd in 2010, Howes was one of her most prominent supporters.

'To each of you who were adopted or removed, who were led to believe your mother had rejected you,' the prime minister continued, as her friend sat crying in front of her, 'and who were denied the opportunity to grow up with your family and community of origin and to connect with your culture, we say sorry.

'We deplore the shameful practices that denied you, the mothers, your fundamental rights and responsibilities to love and care for your children.'

Julia Gillard also lost a friend that day—Simon Crean, who was one of her ministers, and a former Labor and ACTU leader. The two had once been close, even holidaying together with family members. Crean had come to see her the night before, complaining about the way the government was being run. She didn't particularly want to hear it. He had ended the conversation by saying he was contemplating moving a spill for the leadership. A shocked Gillard asked him not to do so before speaking to her again.

Crean did not wait. He gave an on-the-run press conference that morning, opening the door to a leadership challenge—which weighed on Gillard as she delivered the nation's apology. After it, she spoke with Crean, who said he would ask for a spill. He did so as the prime minister listened to others make speeches about adoption. Gillard sacked Crean, then went to question time and announced that she herself would call a spill of the leadership at 4.30 p.m. She then motioned to Tony Abbott and said, 'In the meantime, take your best shot.'

Rudd had been destabilising the government and mounting a case for his return to the leadership, saying that he would not challenge, but was open to being drafted by his colleagues.

At 4.20 p.m. he declared he would not be contesting the leadership spill. No one did.

Gillard and Swan were returned unopposed.

But a day that should have been a triumph had turned into a farce. In the midst of all that, the government admitted defeat and withdrew its media law bills, which had no chance of passing now that the Greens and independents would not back them. A lot of political capital had been expended on the bills, all for nothing.

The whole challenge shemozzle was memorably described by journalist Annabel Crabb as 'a piece of performance art by very confused people'. Treasurer Wayne Swan was utterly dismayed, convinced that this debacle had ensured electoral defeat. The government lost a bevy of ministers, who resigned. 'Here we were trying to bed down two of the biggest reforms of the post-war era [the NDIS and the Gonski education reforms] and we had to put up with this sort of nonsense,' he says.

～

The NDIS legislation had passed, the launch sites were agreed, the states were on board—but one matter was still to be resolved. The one that had always been the biggest problem: funding.

Again, the Productivity Commission's preferred option for funding was via general consolidated revenue. Its less-preferred models were imposing a levy, or having all governments paying into a collective pool and drawing funds from there. It had estimated the NDIS would amount to 4 per cent of total commonwealth spending. If a special levy was introduced, it recommended 'adding an increment to existing marginal tax rates, rather than using different income thresholds or new complex tax schedules'. The commission had found that the current spending on disability services—$2.3 billion from the commonwealth, $4.7 billion from the states—needed an extra $6.5 billion, and it proposed that if all costs were borne by Canberra and the states were no longer paying $4.7 billion, then the states should ease their taxes, such as stamp duties, by a corresponding amount so that people were no worse off.

The funding mechanism was now the subject of many meetings between Gillard, Swan and Macklin. Wayne Swan had been living day in, day out with the GFC since the day he took office. It had become particularly real for him on 10 January 2008, when he was on his annual holiday, on the Sunshine Coast, at Maroochydore. His US counterpart, Hank Paulson, called. Swan was in his car at the local newsagent, having just picked up the morning papers. Queensland rain was beating on the roof. There'd be no surfing for the treasurer this day. Swan jammed the phone between shoulder and ear, stuck a finger in the other ear to drown out the rain, and took notes with the other hand. 'If we can avoid a meltdown in house prices, we can see a way through this,' said Paulson. Big 'if', given that the housing market was where the whole disaster had started.

As he was on holidays, Swan was doing some summer reading, as he recounts in his own book, *The Good Fight*. One of the books he was in the midst of was *Red Ted*, a biography of 'Red Ted' Theodore, another Queensland Labor man, who was sworn in as federal treasurer on 22 October 1929. Two days later came Black Thursday, when the US stock market crashed, generally recognised as the day the Great Depression began. Swan could empathise.

Wayne Swan was no ordinary treasurer, in that he had a great deal of interest and experience in the social ministries, from 1998 to 2004 having been shadow minister for families and community services, the position in which Macklin had succeeded him. That interest culminated in his 2005 book, *Postcode: The Splintering of a Nation*, which argued that the benefits of the boom years of the Howard government had been shared unequally, and that the combination of job insecurity, massive mortgages and an unfair tax system boded ill for the future.

Having come to power at such a difficult time, he was determined to plot a Labor way through the quagmire. Which he did, committing to the biggest-ever increase in the age pension, in 2009, and being the treasurer who introduced the nation's first paid parental leave scheme. 'We did all this amidst the toxicity of the debt and deficit politics, against all that garbage,' Swan says.

In 2010 he had announced that the budget should be in surplus come 2013. It wasn't. Revenue for the year was $12 billion below treasury forecasts—roughly the price of one year of the NDIS. Revenue kept coming in way under treasury's forecasts. They were consistently wrong because something that had never happened before was happening now—nominal growth (the dollar value of production) was consistently less than trend growth. That meant the economy was growing, but government revenues weren't. This was largely because of successful economic policy—the nation's economy was seen as a haven in this time of crisis, which meant that overseas money flooded in, seeking a safe harbour while other currencies were seen as dubious. All that buying of the Australian dollar meant it was high—which meant exports were suffering and imports booming.

That became a political gift for the opposition, even though Australia, meanwhile, had had its credit rating upgraded to AAA by one of the three main agencies, and was already rated AAA by the other two, which had never happened before. In the meantime, the economies of Greece, Italy, Spain, Portugal and Ireland were teetering under unpayable debt, threatening a second wave of the GFC.

These were the circumstances in which Swan was trying to introduce the biggest reform in Australia in forty years. The government had a ready-made excuse to do nothing; it was determined to push on, though.

'I made it absolutely clear the NDIS had to be properly funded—that was non-negotiable,' Swan recalls. 'Jenny and I had decided very early it had to be funded in an enduring and demonstrable way, and it really had to be by the Medicare levy.'

They had looked at all the options. The government's assessment was that the NDIS could definitely not be funded through consolidated revenue, as the Productivity Commission had preferred.

'It was never really in my mind to do it via consolidated revenue; at least as I recall, ten years on without referring to my notes. We couldn't get away with funding it from consolidated revenue. How could you go into an election with an unfunded structural change like that? It's preposterous, just as a matter of political logic, given where we were, and where we were likely to be. Maybe in other circumstances, but not at that time, not in the GFC. Revenue was down, it didn't come back; year after year, it just kept slipping away.'

The government decided to increase the Medicare levy from 1.5 per cent to 2 per cent. That meant an Australian earning an average wage of $70 000 a year would pay about one dollar a day for the NDIS.

Macklin agrees. 'The other big call was the decision to increase the Medicare levy,' she says. 'I'd been on the ERC [Expenditure Review Committee] for all the time in government. I had a big-spending portfolio. I'm an economist by trade. So I knew what the state of the budget was when the question came "How are we going to pay for this?" There were a lot of meetings on this, [with] me and the treasurer and the prime minister. We looked at a lot of options, all the options. In the end, we knew there had to be a tax increase.'

But Gillard had previously ruled out a levy and was wary of the political problems it could present. A levy had actually been suggested to her at another dinner she hosted at the Lodge: for the premiers on the eve of a COAG meeting in July 2012. Queensland's Campbell Newman had raised it, saying a levy could cover the full cost of the NDIS—handily excusing the states from chipping in. 'I smelt a rat,' Gillard wrote in *My Story*. Newman tweeted the next day that she had missed the opportunity to get agreement on NDIS funding. Despite the convention of Chatham House rules applying at the dinner, all the details of it appeared in the papers at the weekend, down to what was served for dessert (chocolate and peanut butter parfait, yum). That was the last time guests at the Lodge received a printed menu.

Gillard was being hounded daily about the so-called carbon tax as well as the aforementioned non-arriving surplus. The political atmosphere was febrile, with Abbott hammering his message day after day: broken promises, new taxes. Everyone remembers his 'axe the tax' slogan.

Despite all efforts at bipartisanship, the disability sector felt sick at the prospect that their whole project could collapse in the midst of this politicking. 'We were afraid that this additional half per cent on the Medicare levy ... would be cast as a big new tax, which it could easily have been,' says Ken Baker.

Gillard bit the bullet on 1 May 2013, did a backflip and said she would raise the Medicare levy to finance the NDIS. It would not cover all costs—some money would come from other savings, some from the states. She stated she would raise the levy after the September election she had already announced.

Predictably, the first question from a journalist was about 'broken promises'. Gillard would have been fortified by polling that said 85 per cent of Australians were in favour of increasing the levy to pay for the scheme.

You could argue, as Macklin does, that the levy increase was not a new tax—'It was an *increase* on an existing tax. We didn't shy away from that. It was one of the options the PC gave us. We just didn't think it could be done from consolidated revenue.'

Everyone expected Abbott to renew his tax scare campaign. Gillard certainly did. He was already 'out there campaigning—already complaining—about the possibility of a new tax,' she said, just a few days later. 'The shadow treasurer was on radio saying it would hurt the economy.'

Indeed, Hockey went on the attack immediately, saying the levy would hit every Australian household. But he was not in alignment with his leader.

Abbott surprised everyone. He didn't oppose it.

Instead, he dared Gillard to introduce it to the parliament immediately. She had the numbers to succeed, even with her minority government.

The Greens were accusing Gillard of cynicism—she could do it now, without Abbott's support, so just do it, they said.

Abbott dared her to introduce the levy rise now, saying, 'If she's fair dinkum, let's get this legislation into the Parliament, and I'm very happy to deal with it in the four [sitting] weeks after the budget.' But he had not said he would support it.

So Gillard double-dared him back.

She said she would introduce it—if he would support it. If he wouldn't, then she would not introduce the legislation, but instead take it to the election, making it an issue for the voters.

With parliament sitting for only four weeks in the meantime, it was a tight squeeze.

Abbott now had to make a choice. He was under pressure *not* to support the increase—by his would-be treasurer, Joe Hockey; by the previous treasurer, Peter Costello; and by others. But he was also under pressure to *support* the levy—from the state premiers, who would have been delighted to see the commonwealth provide extra funds. Four states had conservative premiers: Barnett in Western Australia, Denis Napthine (having ousted Ted Baillieu) in Victoria, O'Farrell in New South Wales, and Newman in Queensland. Then there was the pressure exerted by the disability sector and the tens of thousands of people campaigning for the NDIS, still writing to their local MPs and to the premiers.

Abbott caucused overnight by phone with his shadow cabinet, some of whom were opposed. But there were 2 million Australians who wanted the NDIS—and they would be voting in September. He had been a strong backer of the NDIS for more than a year; if he wavered now, would his support be seen as suspect? On the other hand, if he said no, when campaigning he could say that Labor would raise taxes straightaway with the levy. Then again, polls showed people were in favour of the tax hike.

As it happened, Abbott was doing the annual Pollie Pedal, in which he and others rode bikes, raising funds for charity. That charity was Carers Australia—the very body representing the carers of people with disability. Its head, Ara Cresswell, was riding alongside him.

Cresswell had been mobilising the troops, getting people out to persuade Abbott and the other politicians on the ride. This was the Every Australian Counts campaign in action, now with another slogan: 'Make It Real'.

'We worked with local carers groups, we bussed them in, we did everything we could to get those families out. The bike ride was raising funds for Carers Australia and I wanted everyone on that ride to understand what that meant. I wanted them to know that when we talk about carers, we are not talking about paid workers, we are talking about families who would give their eyeteeth to make sure their family member got the best possible outcome. At every stop, we had people there to meet with the bike riders. At morning teas and lunches, they would speak and tell their story. I will never forget a woman telling her heartbreaking story about looking after her husband with his chronic illness and her two children with autism, and seeing these grown men weep. That was our aim—to make sure those people understand what the cause was, and to go a step bigger: the NDIS.'

It is with great pride that Ara Cresswell remembers—as do so many others—Tony Abbott getting off his bike and saying, *Yes, if Julia Gillard introduces the levy legislation now, I will support it.* Gillard did. He did too.

Just like that, the biggest obstacle that had stood in the way of the rights of people with disability was removed.

It was a win for everybody. Gillard had what she wanted—and knew this grand achievement would outlive her government if it fell at the election. Abbott had neutralised an issue that could have been used against him in the campaign. He would not have to increase the levy himself, and was seen to be supporting something, not just being negative.

Most importantly, people with disability and their families could suddenly see a secure foundation for the NDIS into the future.

It was also a win for Every Australian Counts. 'The public affairs campaign objective was to influence the public first,' says John Della Bosca, 'and the public would change the politicians' minds because they would feel it was legit. And that was the contest between Julia and Tony—who could go more NDIS than the other—and that contest was set up because we achieved an overwhelming public sentiment in favour of reform, and that the NDIS was the appropriate reform. And, you know, in some ways I amazed myself because I would never have believed it could have been that successful, but it was.'

Gillard's move ensured that support for the NDIS funding was bipartisan. That had been fundamental to Every Australian Counts. As Bonyhady says: 'The NDIS has had a much less contested history than Medicare. And I credit the EAC campaign for that.

'One of the things that's really fantastic about this scheme is that it has been able to be bipartisan,' Bonyhady continues, 'to be across all governments, that it has endured across leadership changes, across ministerial changes. The idea and the reality are so powerful that it has been embraced successfully. Our aim was always to have this scheme stand side by side with Medicare, as a real pillar of fairness and decency on which Australia is built—to be unmovable, part of the core infrastructure as part of Australian society. And I think we've got that.'

Abbott, by this time, had been raising funds for carers for several years on his Pollie Pedal bike ride, and after five years, they totalled in the millions. The experience was eye-opening, as he and Cresswell recount.

'When I came in to Carers Australia, I was told we would be the recipient of Tony Abbott's Pollie Pedal fundraising,' Cresswell recalls. 'I was a little worried. When we first met, I think we looked at each other and thought, *This is never going to work*. By the end, I gained an enormous respect for him. In the process, he met countless people with disability, and countless families. He was extraordinary with several of them. I saw a side of him that people don't get to see, which I came to admire. We are vastly different, him and I, but I came to have enormous respect for the way that he treated people. He really gained an understanding of people whose lives rotate around disability. I take my hat off to him. That's the thing about finding common ground. It took going out on the road with a whole lot of middle-aged, conservative men in lycra to really understand they are good people too, we just do it differently. They took the issues to heart.'

Several months later, Abbott, by this time prime minister, would speak at the National Press Club, launching Carers Week, where he was introduced by Cresswell.

'I am proud that one very good thing at least has come from the last parliament and that is the foundation of our National Disability Insurance Scheme, because despite all the difficulties of the last three years, despite all of the partisanship, we were able to come together and agree that the National Disability Insurance Scheme was an idea whose time had come, that a decent society owed it to our most vulnerable to give them a new deal and a better deal.

'I'm pleased that the Coalition supported the National Disability Insurance Scheme every step of the way. We supported the proposed Productivity Commission inquiry when the new Opposition Leader, then the Parliamentary Secretary, Bill Shorten, proposed this back in 2010. We welcomed and supported the Productivity Commission report when it came out. We voted through the Parliament the enabling legislation and we supported the levy which will substantially if not totally fund the National Disability Insurance Scheme.

'I may not have spoken this way—if I may speak candidly with you—even a few years ago, because a few years ago I hadn't been brought into contact with the world of caring, as I have been over the last few years through Carers Australia and the Pollie Pedal ... We haven't just been raising money. In all of the towns and villages and communities along the way, thanks to the work of Carers Australia, we have been meeting with and mixing with carers and those they care for. It's humbling because you realise the difficult circumstances that so many Australians face. It's daunting because you ask yourself, "What would I do if I was confronted with something like this?" But it's inspiring because you see how many people rise so magnificently to meet the challenges of life. No one knows what the future holds. No one knows what fate has in store for us.'

∽

Only a few short weeks after the levy dare and double-dare, treasurer Wayne Swan got to stand and deliver his budget speech, which he was certain would be his last.

'Labor chooses a stronger, smarter and fairer Australia,' he said.

'An Australia where our schoolchildren get the opportunity to reach their full potential with $9.8 billion invested in new school funding.

'An Australia which gives dignity to people with severe and permanent disability through the historic $14.3 billion investment in DisabilityCare Australia. This is a proud moment for our country.

'An Australia where our prosperity spreads opportunity to every postcode in our nation.'

Which brings us to an odd little story—about the name 'DisabilityCare'. It was coined to chime with 'Medicare', to subtly communicate the idea that the schemes were consonant, part of each other, as Gillard referenced at Noah's Ark, and as intended by Bonyhady. Macklin says it was also coined because 'people with disability didn't really like the word "insurance" because they associated that with insurance companies—and it's hard to explain the notion of social insurance. So we called it DisabilityCare. And also to show the relationship with the other big social insurance scheme, Medicare.'

It turns out people with disability disliked this name even more— the scheme was about a lot more than care. Many did not need care at all. The new Liberal government would change the name immediately. They justified this by research that showed clearly the sector hated the name—but many believe their priority was to cleave the association with Medicare, which remains a sore point for the party. It famously dismantled Whitlam's Medibank. After Bob Hawke reinstated it as Medicare in 1984, the Liberals kept promising they would get rid of it again, and kept losing elections. Only when John Howard promised not to do so in 1996 did they get re-elected. Which goes some way towards explaining prime minister Malcolm Turnbull's fury on the night of the 2016 election, when he vowed to get the police to investigate the 'Mediscare' text messages that claimed his government would be privatising Medicare.

Macklin had brought a $14 billion proposition to the ERC—not something that happens every day—and the treasurer had approved it. In a light moment, Macklin asked Swan why he had. 'Because you recommended it,' he joked. Swan is a funnier man than you might suspect. The two are good friends—'policy soulmates', says Swan—who had put in the hard yards and the long hours examining every line of government expenditure for six long years.

There's no mistaking his respect for her. 'You didn't have to be an expert on the NDIS or disability if you were confident that Jenny Macklin had a grasp on it,' he says.

The $14 billion was the allocation for the NDIS for 2013–14. The Medicare levy was for the years thereafter. The legislation for it was introduced the next day by Prime Minister Gillard. Ken Baker was there that day, and even though his confidence that the NDIS would eventuate had been growing month by month for years, even now he still feared bipartisanship might fail and it could fall at the last hurdle. In the end, this day became one that everyone remembers—for one thing.

It was the day Gillard cried.

She began confidently. 'Australia's strong economy and Australia's social safety nets are the envy of the world. In this bill, we see Australia at its very best,' she said.

She pointed out how this was collective action, pooling resources to do what individuals alone can't do, and that it was politics actually working, 'a united embrace of national responsibility ... DisabilityCare will be here when you need it—election after election, decade after decade, generation after generation.'

She outlined the legislation, then told two stories. The first was about being in Melbourne two weeks earlier to sign up Victoria to the NDIS. At the media event, Sophie Deane, a little girl who liked to climb on monkey bars and take photos, a little girl with Down syndrome, asked to take the prime minister's picture. She did so. Sophie is the daughter of Kirsten Deane. A week later, Gillard was in Brisbane signing up Queensland, and met Sandy, a young man with a condition resembling cerebral palsy. He handed her a thankyou card with her photo on it—the one taken by Sophie.

'In years to come, DisabilityCare Australia will ensure Sophie and Sandy and so many other young people with disability will have the security and dignity every Australian deserves,' she told the House.

Then Gillard's voice cracked as she said, 'This, above all, is why Australians are so overwhelmingly supportive of DisabilityCare.'

She struggled to make it through. 'Over the past six years, the idea of a National Disability Insurance Scheme has found a place in our nation's hearts. In March, we gave it a place in our nation's laws. Today we inscribe it in our nation's finances.'

Faltering, she said, 'There will be no more "in principle' and no more "when circumstances permit". There will be ... permanent care, not temporary help.'

Barely able to get the words out, the prime minister concluded: 'DisabilityCare starts in seven weeks' time, and there will be no turning back.'

The phrase 'there will be no turning back' was the same one uttered by Macklin after the release of *Shut Out* and all the tales it told. The women were not for turning.

When Gillard took her seat, after a hug from Macklin, Swan leaned over and said, 'I would have had my money on Macklin doing the crying.'

Once again, the opposition benches were all but empty, Kevin Andrews being an exception. 'I congratulate the government for having brought this forward,' he said.

ᔑ

DisabilityCare did start in seven weeks' time—but Julia Gillard was no longer prime minister.

When the parliament sat in June for its last two weeks before the September election, Gillard felt she would not be leader at the end of the session. She was right.

On parliament's second-last day, she lost a leadership ballot to Kevin Rudd. Wayne Swan was out too. Which meant the two of them were backbenchers the next day, her last day in parliament. As they entered the chamber, Gillard asked Swan where their seats were. 'It's all fine. Near Dick Adams. We just need to look for him.' Adams is a very big man who stands out in a crowd, but just to make things worse, he was absent from the chamber.

So it was that when the NDIS came into being four days later, the honour of opening the Newcastle office on 1 July 2013 fell to Kevin Rudd.

Meanwhile, the photo of Julia Gillard that hangs in the Museum of Australian Democracy at Old Parliament House, the photo on her Twitter feed, is the one taken by Sophie Deane.

WHAT IT TOOK

———

WHAT DID IT take to make the NDIS a reality?

Well, it took more than a hundred years since future prime minister Joseph Cook first said Australia must have such a scheme.

It took more than forty years for Gough Whitlam's legislation to be resuscitated.

It took the serendipity of people in government circles in New South Wales—John Della Bosca and John Walsh—to be thinking in these terms at the same time that Bruce Bonyhady and Brian Howe and Bronwyn Morkham were doing the same in Victoria, just as a new government came to power in Canberra. It took Bill Shorten to bring all these strands together—to turn a good idea into a working proposal, a detailed case, an argument so tight, so well thought out, so substantiated with data and costings and projections, that it could persuade the economic hard heads of the Productivity Commission.

But in politics, you must win hearts as well as minds, and Shorten knew that too, and so there was the creation first of a ministerial council that brought together the warring factions of the disability sector, and then of an Alliance that truly united them, both headed by Rhonda Galbally. Thus, a previously insoluble political problem was solved: there had been no votes in disability; once the sector united, it could hardly be opposed.

That became clear once everyday Australians mobilised in great numbers to demand their NDIS. When it was aligned with Medicare, the rest of the country saw its fairness and supported a tax rise to pay for it. That fusion with Medicare was the key to unlocking the finances, to which every government and party agreed—all the more remarkable during a time of extreme partisanship in the nation's politics. Justice Michael Kirby had long ago said better economic times would need to come before Whitlam's idea could be revived—as it turned out, it came back to life during the worst economic times.

That such a scheme, so enormous in cost, size and effect, came from an idea regenerated outside government and was then, in the first instance, drawn up by a group outside government—the DIG team—driven by an MP who was not even a minister, is some sort of political miracle. But miracles don't just happen: they are made.

Stories typically have one hero. This story has many.

For the NDIS to come into being, it took the heroic work of the disability activists in the 1970s and 1980s—Lesley Hall and her comrades—to convey the notion that they had rights.

It took the efforts of the Hawke–Keating government to start the process of creating the space in Australian society for those with disability, once they had been released from the institutions that held them.

It took the creativity of Gough Whitlam to see that the law of negligence was an abomination and that the space needed to be occupied by a universal insurance scheme.

It took the inquiring mind of Brian Howe, still researching social policy in his seventies and beyond, to dust off an old idea.

It took the perseverance of Senator Jan McLucas, and the other members of her Senate committee, to get that chamber to inquire in depth into the deficiencies of the system.

It took the grandiosity of Kevin Rudd to create a platform at the Australia 2020 Summit to give this idea a stage on which to shine.

It took the smarts of Bruce Bonyhady and Helen Sykes to seize that opportunity, prompted by Bonyhady's response to a migrant mother pleading for help for her child.

It took the spunk of Gina Anderson to make the case for the NDIS at the summit in the couple of minutes available to her.

It took the dedication and relentlessness of Rhonda Galbally over so many years, in so many ways, not to let this opportunity slip away.

It took the nous of John Della Bosca to mount a campaign that resonated with Australians.

It took Peter, James, Claire, Robert and Mary, and Billie to share their stories on the Every Australian Counts website.

It took Lyn, carting her card table to the supermarket every day to get shoppers to sign the NDIS petition.

It took the perspicacity of John Walsh to investigate the concept of an NDIS long after Whitlam's idea had faded from consciousness and long before anyone else had revisited it.

It took the economic intelligence and patience of Bonyhady, Ian Silk, Bill Moss, John Walsh, Helen Hambling and the other members of DIG, and the people at PwC, to gather the data and crunch the numbers to show that this thing could work.

It took the staunchness of many thousands of Australians with disability to tell their stories and demand their rights. They had to do it repeatedly in their daily lives; they did it in publicly repeatedly, too, in forums in the 1970s, for *New Directions* in the 1980s, to the Senate inquiry in 2006, for *Shut Out* in 2009, for Every Australian Counts, to the Productivity Commission, and even after the legislation was introduced. It took the thousands more who turned up to rallies and petitioned their local MPs. It took the nearly 200 000 who said 'Count me in' on the Every Australian Counts website.

It took the clear-sightedness of Bill Shorten to see the problems when he took up his role, it took his moral sense to be outraged by them, and it took his political genius and strategic thinking to create the groups that drove its acceptance.

It took the open mind of Jenny Macklin to support her junior; then her determination, political skill and policy savvy to take command of the idea, marshal it through the treacherous waters of politics, then lead it through the tortuous tracks of multi-level negotiation to its ultimate home, the parliament.

It took the intelligence and empathy of Productivity Commissioner Patricia Scott to recognise a good idea and a just cause when presented with one.

It took the diligence of the public service, from Ian Watt and Jeff Harmer down, to do all the work—the submissions, the negotiations, the legislation—to turn an idea into a reality.

It took the combined courage of prime minister Julia Gillard and treasurer Wayne Swan to overcome the politics of the day to prioritise the politics of the future, to bite the bullet, and fund the scheme with a tax increase combined with spending savings.

It took the wherewithal of Tony Abbott not to stand in the way and seek political advantage as his predecessors had done—as some of his colleagues and ex-colleagues urged him to do—and his humbleness to accede to the pleas of the people.

It took the humanity of one little girl, Sophie Deane, and her camera to make the story so clear for so many who otherwise might not have given the problem a thought. It took Sophie's grandmother telling her book club about this idea, and it took years of work by Sophie's mum, Kirsten Deane. (Sophie, by the way, is doing well, having finished school, found part-time office work, and started a business with friends making and selling tote bags. And Bruce Bonyhady reports his boys are thriving, living independently with a friend.)

It took the good sense of the Australian people to consider the proposal and say, *Yes, this is the right thing to do, and we are prepared to pay for it. It is for all of us.*

Above all, it took love.

It took the love of parents caring for their children—when others saw the extent of their love, they wanted to help.

It took the love of all the people mentioned above, who wanted to do something to make other people's lives better.

It took the love of the Australian people for their compatriots to agree that *Yes, we shall do this.*

It is the biggest and greatest thing that Australia has done in the past half-century—and it was conceived, campaigned for and built mainly by people with disability. It has transformed more than half a million people's lives, from being objects of charity and pity, excluded from society, to being citizens fully engaged in life.

The NDIS is something we should all be proud of. It is something we need to protect.

INDEX

———